GOOD FOOD
MADE SIMPLE

GOOD FOOD MADE SIMPLE

HEALTHY RECIPES TO EAT WELL AND FEEL INCREDIBLE

LEAH ITSINES

murdoch books

Sydney | London

CONTENTS

{

Introduction

Thank you for picking up this book – I truly appreciate the support and I am eternally grateful that you're allowing me to share with you my love and passion for food. Buckle in for some seriously delicious, nutritious and incredibly satisfying food that's healthy but doesn't compromise on taste – ever!

I come from a really big Greek family where food was always at the forefront of our gatherings. It was all about whose yiayia (grandmother) was bringing the pita and whose papou (grandfather) was on the barbecue. There was inevitably a ridiculous number of cousins, which meant the volume of our parties was quite loud, to say the least. And I wouldn't have had it any other way because this taught me the meaning of food – that food is a celebration, a gift that we are given every day, and to make the most of it. I also learned how good food can taste when it's made from the most basic of ingredients (my yiayia grew most of her ingredients – she's a wizard, I swear).

My aim in this book, and in my career, is to make food easy and to help people look at food in a positive way. If you don't feel confident in the kitchen because you haven't had much practice, or you fear food due to a bad relationship with it, I desperately want to change those views and help you push forward.

The biggest trend I've noticed in the online world is that people are becoming more aware of their health. While there's more noise than ever about what's best for your health, people are finally catching on that an understanding of nutrition basics is all you need not only to survive, but to seriously thrive.

I'll first take you through some basic nutritional fundamentals that I believe are a really great start to making healthy changes in your life, then introduce you to some cooking basics and where to start. I'll give you my tips for making the most of your freezer and show you how meal prepping can make life easier. Then we're onto the pantry and I'll quickly drop past and organise it for you … just kidding, but I will tell you how to do it so you're not overbuying or shoving things into places where you'll never find them! After we're done there, it's onto the incredible recipes I've developed to get you into the kitchen and seriously loving it.

There's something special about being 'in' people's homes, bringing families together with something they can hold, get dirty or pass on. So please, keep this book in your kitchen, get it dirty and use it in your everyday cooking. I'm ready to get cooking … are you?

Let's do this!

Leah xx

Food fundamentals

It's probably no surprise that I love healthy eating – it's everything I live and breathe! However, I didn't always make the healthiest of choices. When I was in high school, I went from eating a healthy Mediterranean diet of home-cooked meals to something a lot less nutritious – takeaway meals, alcohol, and so on. I became unwell and knew I needed to make a change, and I started by changing my eating habits. I came up with my own list of fundamentals about food and nutrition, which really helped me, and I still swear by it to this day. If you're new to healthy eating, it's important to know that a healthy change is never linear – you'll have ups and downs because change is hard. But using my food fundamentals, you can do it and your body will love you for it.

1. BALANCE

Balance is key. One thing I want you to grasp is that balance is the key to healthy change. If you can't see yourself sticking to something for the rest of your life, or it makes you miserable or doesn't suit you and your lifestyle, ask yourself, 'Is it worth it?' If it's not and you don't like it, then it's not for you. This is how I feel about hardcore dieting and being strict with food. Coming from a big Greek family, I love food, so I much prefer a balanced outlook that suits my lifestyle. When it comes to nutrition, it's important to listen to your body, especially around cravings and what your body is wanting. Enjoying every meal and eating to fuel yourself is what life should be all about. Your relationship with food will get better the more you listen to your body, its needs and your hunger cues, and actually replenish it with what you're craving. Balance is my key ingredient to success when looking to make a healthy change.

2. BE REALISTIC

Being realistic goes hand in hand with balance. Creating a realistic lifestyle and relationship with food is important for your long-term success – be realistic when you're making changes. If you've never meal prepped (see pages 14–17) before, it would be a big leap to attempt to prepare a week's worth of meals in 2 hours on a Sunday. Not only is this unrealistic, but it can be quite overwhelming. A more realistic approach would be to spend time on a Saturday creating a meal plan and shopping list for the week ahead, buying those ingredients and then preparing one or two ingredients on the Sunday. You could start by making a couple of snacks for the week, gradually working your way up to meal prepping more and more meals every week. It's important to ask, 'Am I feeling comfortable with this? Can I keep this up?' and then build or reduce your load from there.

3. VARIETY

Variety is everything. It's important to include a variety of different proteins, carbohydrates and fats in your meals to keep your food exciting. Typically I eat a bunch of different meats, seafoods, vegetables, pastas, grains, salads and fruits – that's what truly allows me to have a balanced diet. Every time I'm developing a recipe or coming up with meals for my family, I ask myself, 'What else can I add to this?' This is what really helps keep my meals exciting – no two meals are ever the same and I'm always enjoying a range of foods each day. (Granted, my additions are typically olives or artichokes, but that's beside the point!) Choosing a variety of ingredients also means you're adding different macro and micro nutrients into your body, which provides different key nutrients, and it will mean you never get bored with your food. Hot tip from me: make your food more exciting. Food should never be boring or bland!

4. SIMPLICITY

Simplicity is important. I believe that good food is always simple, so make sure you pick simple ingredients that pack a punch with flavour. You don't need to work away in the kitchen for hours on end just to put a meal on the table (although I sometimes love to do this). Simple ingredients and simple recipes are always a win. Read on for my tips on organising your pantry (pages 19–20) and using spices (pages 22–23), and see pages 24– 35 for some easy marinades – these will help you use simple ingredients to make incredible meals.

5. CELEBRATE AND SHARE

It's good to celebrate and share your wins and, of course, the amazing food you've made. For me, cooking is always more enjoyable when I'm able to share my creations with other people. You could be perfecting your mum's spaghetti meatball recipe, or trying a new recipe that makes you look like a *MasterChef* winner in front of your family. Food should always be a celebration, and the art of cooking is a skill to embrace and celebrate, especially when you nail a recipe. My family often see me giving myself a pat on the back when I have success, and you should do the same!

Balance is my key ingredient to success

Mix it up!

It's easy to get into a rut of buying the same ingredients because they're in your comfort zone, but think about how much deliciousness you could be missing out on! I'm all about flexibility, and I want you to be confident to swap ingredients you don't like with things you love. Getting more variety in your diet is always a good thing, too.

These lists are designed to inspire you to try something new, but they're just the beginning. Spend time exploring the aisles of your supermarket or greengrocer, or visit a farmers' market – you might surprise yourself and find your new favourite food!

PROTEIN

- Chicken, turkey or duck breast
- Lean beef or lamb
- Minced meat
- Fish (fresh or tinned)
- Prawns
- Lentils, beans or chickpeas (tinned or dried)
- Eggs (chicken or duck)
- Tofu (firm or soft)
- Tempeh
- Hard cheeses

FRUITS

- Berries: blueberries, raspberries, blackberries
- Banana
- Orange
- Pear
- Pineapple
- Watermelon
- Kiwifruit
- Grapes
- Stone fruit: peach, nectarine, plum, apricot
- Frozen fruit
- Tinned fruit (no added sugar)

CEREALS AND GRAINS

- Bread
- Rice (brown, jasmine, basmati, white)
- Noodles (hokkien, vermicelli)
- Pasta (wholemeal or regular)
- Barley
- Buckwheat
- Couscous
- Oats
- Quinoa flakes
- Rice bubbles

VEGETABLES

- Leafy greens: spinach, rocket (arugula), kale, silverbeet (Swiss chard)
- Starchy veggies: potato, corn, sweet potato
- Green veggies: broccoli, capsicum (pepper), zucchini (courgette), peas
- Orange veggies: carrot, pumpkin (squash)

Love your freezer

I never used to use my freezer properly, partly because I didn't know how long foods would last or how to properly thaw them. It was all too confusing! However, after a few trials and errors, I've grown to love my freezer and all the goodness it provides.

Here are my top tips on using your freezer to its fullest potential, with a little cheat sheet to help you work out how long you can store different foods.

ROTATE: Each month, or every couple of months, ensure you check inside your freezer. (Sometimes I put things in there and forget about them, then it's like a present to myself when I find soup a couple of months later.) Regularly rotate your freezer and plan meals around what you have already prepared.

LABEL: Whenever you freeze something you've cooked, write on the container what it is and the date you made it so that you know when it needs to be eaten.

COVER: Always cover or tightly wrap food to ensure it doesn't get freezer burn (the icy bits!). I freeze food in reusable containers with airtight lids or reusable bags with resealable zips.

PORTION: I recommend freezing meals in single or double portions. That way, you can pull out only what you need and minimise wastage – there's no point pulling out a batch of pasta sauce that will feed six if you're only cooking for one or two.

THAW: The safest way to thaw anything is in the fridge overnight. Alternatively, you can thaw food in the microwave using the defrost setting. However, this can quickly bring meat into the 'danger zone', so if you're going to do this, cook the meat immediately once it has been thawed. The 'danger zone' is a temperature that's a great breeding ground for bacteria, which is anything above 5°C (41°F) up to 60°C (140°F). This is why the safest place to thaw frozen food is in the fridge.

When you're reheating food, the general rule of thumb is to reheat it in the same way it was originally cooked. For example, reheating your pizza in the oven will result in a better texture than reheating it in the microwave, which will make the pizza soggy. However, if you only have a microwave available, the way you reheat your food is still important. If you're heating more than one type of food, such as rice, vegetables and meat, you may need to stagger the heating process. The meat will take longer to heat than the rice, so you'll need to put this in first, then follow it with the vegetables and rice to ensure everything is ready at the same time.

Food storage cheat sheet

FOOD	MAXIMUM FREEZING TIME
Raw meat and poultry	4–6 months (my preference – can be longer)
Cooked meat and poultry	2–3 months
Raw fish	3 months (my preference – can be longer)
Vegetables	4–6 months
Fruit	3 months
Soups	3 months
Sauces	4–6 months
Breads, wraps and pizza bases	3–6 months
Baked goods (muffins, pastries, etc.)	1–2 months
Egg items (quiches, frittatas, etc.)	1–2 months

Meal prepping

Meal prepping has been a game changer for me, and I encourage you to try it, too. It's something I choose to do every week (and have for a couple of years) because it makes my life much easier throughout the week. That means I can prioritise other things, such as my family and wellbeing, instead of having to rush home to cook dinner. Meal prepping is not essential when you're reaching for healthy change, but it does make life a lot easier and, in my opinion, is pivotal.

I'm sure you've had a conversation with either your partner or yourself along these lines: 'What do you want for dinner? ... No, I don't feel like that ... Okay, well you choose!' It may go on that way for an hour or so before you finally settle on something, by which time you're rushing and dinner becomes more of a stressful chore than a time to relax and enjoy. When people hear 'meal prep' they often think of boring prepared meals (like plain chicken, rice and broccoli) and having to prepare your entire weekly menu from scratch – but for me, this isn't the case. It just means being better prepared in the kitchen so that it's easier to whip up dinner.

I prefer to cook 'fresh' every night (with a little help from meal prep!), and that works well for me, but you need to find what works for you. That could be organising your pantry so it's easier to find what you're looking for, writing a meal plan, rearranging your fridge, checking what you have in the freezer, chopping up ingredients and/or cooking some components of meals (such as sauces, marinades, stocks, broths, etc.). Meal prepping is an effective strategy if you are time poor or you simply don't enjoy cooking every day. If you haven't tried meal prepping before, welcome to this incredible world! I've broken it down for you over the next couple of pages to help you get started.

Meal prep is what YOU make it!

WHAT FOOD CAN I PREPARE?

There are many foods you can prepare as a part of your meal prep, but I prefer to make some foods fresh. You can prepare any food that stores well in the refrigerator, but that also keeps its taste, texture and smell after a few days, such as cooked meats, vegetables, soups and grains. These are all easy to prepare and will be absolutely fine in the fridge.

The meals I avoid preparing in advance are meals that won't last more than a couple of hours after they've been served. For example, I wouldn't try to prepare a salad that would be extremely soggy after being dressed. Nachos wouldn't stay crispy and you risk eating a very sad meal two to three days later. In these cases, I'd just prepare parts of the meal, such as the guacamole (with lemon juice squeezed over the top to prevent it turning brown) and the bean mixture, and then assemble it 'fresh' on the night.

Figuring out what works will be more or less trial and error – but that's exactly how you learn and progress.

SCHEDULE A TIME

When you think of meal prep, do you think of hours in the supermarket and kitchen on a Sunday? I used to, too, until I found a really good way of splitting the 'work' so that it was much less overwhelming and I could complete tasks one by one and still enjoy my weekend.

Here's how I split up the workload – maybe it would work for you?

FRIDAY

Meal plan and shopping lists: I meal plan on my lunchbreak at work on Fridays, choosing all my meals for the week and creating a shopping list at the same time. This makes it easier for me to get up and go shopping on Saturday morning, without having to think about it.

Split up the workload!

SATURDAY

Grocery shopping: I do all of my grocery shopping, then come home and pack it away until the next day. This means I can enjoy the rest of my Saturday.

WEDNESDAY

Grocery shopping (if needed): I grab any fresh items I need for the rest of the week, such as breads, fresh herbs and minced meats.

Meal prep: I spend 1 hour after dinner preparing anything I need for Thursday to Saturday – it's similar to what I do on Sunday, just preparing small components of the meals.

SUNDAY

Meal prep: I do some prep for the dinners I will be eating on Monday, Tuesday and Wednesday. This usually involves marinating or crumbing meats and preparing foods such as tzatziki or meatballs. I tend to prepare and cook vegetables on the day, but I may chop up some of the 'harder' vegetables such as pumpkin, cauliflower, broccoli and carrots, and leave those in the fridge.

This way of meal prepping is my favourite as it breaks it up, making the workload a lot more achievable and there's no need to spend hours prepping at a time. You can do whatever suits you.

Pantry

I love organising the pantry – it's probably one of my favourite things to do because once it's done, I feel so good. I used to just throw things into the pantry and close the door really quickly, and whoever opened it next ... it was their problem! But now, my pantry is my prized possession, and I absolutely love how organised and functional it is – no more wondering if I have a certain ingredient or digging through to the back of the shelves, knocking over everything in my path.

JARS AND LABELS

Tightly sealed jars or containers: these are a worthwhile investment. They don't need to be glass, they just need to have good suction to keep your ingredients fresh. The jars can be different sizes to suit what you're storing. For example, spice jars should be small and compact, whereas pasta or flour jars can be much bigger so they hold a large quantity. I prefer to purchase the same style of containers so that everything looks the same – neat and tidy.

Labels: you can either make these yourself or, if you want to be a little fancy, buy your labels online – you can even pick the font. Having clear labels on your main items helps keep everything well organised. When you empty a packet into a jar, write the use-by date on a small piece of paper and stick it to the bottom of the jar. Then, when the jar is empty, you can rip it off and start again.

SECTIONS/SPACE SAVERS

I have so much fun using space savers and sections in my pantry to make everything look super organised.

Sections: I suggest using medium-sized boxes for 'sectioning' ingredients (such as baking goods, curry pastes, chilli oils, etc.). This means you can put any 'overflow' ingredients into sections to keep them organised.

Three-tier shelving: this allows you to save space by stacking smaller items such as spice jars, making it easier to see and find them rather than being hidden behind larger items. These are also great for tinned goods and items that you want to find easily. You'll find them in most storage shops.

Lazy Susans: these are fantastic for bottled goods, such as oils, sauces and vinegars. Instead of trying to grab a bottle from the back and knocking over every one in front, do a little spin to find the bottle and grab it with ease.

ORGANISE BY CATEGORIES

If you organise your pantry by categories, it's much easier to find what you're looking for. When you're baking a cake, you know to look for sugar or cacao in the baking section; when you're making a curry, you know that you'll find curry paste in the sauces section.

HERE'S HOW I CATEGORISE MY PANTRY:

- **Tinned and long-life goods:** tinned fish, tinned legumes, crushed tomatoes, tinned vegetables, tinned soups, chicken and vegetable stocks, tomato passata (puréed tomatoes), noodle packets, etc.

- **Bulk goods:** rice, flour, pasta, breadcrumbs, etc. (in large containers)

- **Oils and sauces:** oils, vinegars, sauces, curry pastes – these are great in their own section, or you can use a lazy Susan to organise them

- **Baking:** sugars, cacao, baking powder, desiccated coconut, food colourings, cupcake cases, etc.

- **Nuts and seeds:** I need a nut and seed section of its own, but you could combine this with baking or snacks

- **Spices:** I use three-tier racks that prop up the spices so I can easily reach what I need

- **Spreads:** peanut butter, tahini, honey, maple syrup, etc. (these could also go in the baking section, depending on how often you use them)

- **Snacks:** I keep all the protein balls, popcorn, chips, etc. in this section (and usually in an easy-grab spot!)

- **Overflow/extras:** this is a couple of boxes of bits and pieces that are left over from pouring into containers, such as extra flour and rice.

Keep snacks in an easy-grab spot!

Spice your life

I'm all for using spices and making food as delicious as possible, but I'm also passionate about not buying a spice to use once and then have it live out its life in the back of the pantry. Here are the essential spices that I think you need to absolutely nail some recipes. I've given some guidance on how you would typically use them, as well as some notes on my own personal preferences.

INGREDIENT	HOW TO USE IT	LEAH'S TIPS
Salt	Salt is my jam, and I use it to flavour everything. It can really draw out flavour and make those 'boring' or plain foods much more palatable. Don't skip the salt!	I love using salt flakes as I find it easier to judge the amount I'm using. Don't fear salt – having salt as part of a healthy, balanced diet is okay (and delicious).
Pepper	Pepper is like a silent assassin – it doesn't bring really deep heat like chilli does, but it does give a little kick. Pair it with salt – they're basically twins, so you can't use one and not the other.	I love coarsely ground black pepper – it's easy to see and judge how much I'm using, and I find it gives a really deep flavour. Pepper is known to give you a sneezing fit ... avoid taking a big breath when you're sprinkling!
Chilli flakes	These are a great little topper for meals if you don't like a great deal of heat, but want a little bit. You can add chilli flakes at the start of cooking (instead of fresh chilli) or sprinkle them on your finished dishes.	I typically use chilli flakes as either a topper, or as a last resort if I don't have fresh chilli. Keeping these in your pantry is good in case you need a little heat!
Paprika	Paprika adds a vibrant colour to your meals, as well as a slightly sweet taste.	I use smoked paprika in marinades to bring out a deep red colour and add a smoky flavour.

Cinnamon	Cinnamon is a delicious addition to sweet recipes such as porridge, overnight oats, smoothies and pancakes, but it's also delicious in stews, pasta sauces and slow-cooked meals.	I put cinnamon in my ragu pasta sauce and I will never go back! That little hint of cinnamon is something people absolutely love. Try adding it to your meals – you only need a little bit to make a big bang!
Oregano	Dried oregano is perfect with many different proteins – it's one of my favourites to add to a marinade.	I add dried oregano to my pasta sauces, marinades and proteins. I get my oregano from my yiayia's garden and she dries it for me – maybe that explains why I love it so much!
Cumin	Ground cumin has a strong, earthy flavour that pairs really well with Indian-style dishes and is perfect for adding some depth to marinades.	Cumin tastes amazing, but it can be overpowering, so be light with your sprinkles and taste before adding more.
Cayenne pepper	Cayenne pepper packs a punch with heat, so use it with caution! It's a great spice to add to your marinades if you don't have any fresh chilli, or if you want some deep heat.	I always start with $\frac{1}{8}$ teaspoon of this stuff and add more from there – it can very quickly go from a good heat to a fire-breathing type of heat.
Garlic powder	This is great for marinades, and good for people who don't like a really strong garlic flavour. It has more of a sweet and subtle taste, and you don't need to use a lot of it.	I'm a self-confessed garlic queen, so I use fresh garlic where possible. However, I use garlic powder in dishes where it's nicer if the garlic isn't visible.
Onion powder	Similar to garlic powder, this is great for marinades and good for people who don't like a really strong onion flavour.	You only need 1 tablespoon of onion powder to replace 1 whole onion! Add this slowly, because it can overpower a dish.

Marinating your protein and freezing is a great way to save time (and mess!)

MAKE-IT-SIMPLE MARINADES

}

A fancy marinade (made with non-fancy ingredients) is a simple way to add variety to your week and it creates so many options that I never get bored. Buying the protein in bulk packs also keeps the cost down. I've listed the marinades under the protein I would use with them, but some can be used on other proteins as well – go ahead and experiment!

Each of the marinades on the following pages makes enough to coat 1 kg (2 lb 4 oz) of protein, but you can adjust the marinade to match the amount of protein you're using. As a guide, this amount of protein will serve about 4 to 6 people.

Chicken marinades

Garlic
tomato

Teriyaki

Chilli lime
tofu

Sweet and smoky barbecue

Greek
(see page 34)

RECIPES OVER PAGE

Chicken marinades

Suitable for breasts and thighs (bone in or out), wings, legs, kebabs and tofu steaks.

Add all of the marinade ingredients to a bowl and mix well. Pour the marinade over 1 kg (2 lb 4 oz) chicken or tofu steaks and marinate in the fridge for at least 1 hour, preferably overnight. (Tofu needs to be pressed to draw out the excess liquid before marinating. I love to marinate it overnight and then air fry it to make it extra crispy.)

Drain the marinated chicken or tofu and cook it on a hot barbecue or chargrill pan until cooked through.

Teriyaki

½ cup (125 ml) soy sauce
⅓ cup (80 ml) oyster sauce
2 tablespoons honey, warmed
2 tablespoons grated ginger
4 garlic cloves, crushed
2 small red chillies, finely diced (optional)

Tip: For a vegetarian meal, use mushroom oyster sauce.

Sweet and smoky barbecue

⅓ cup (80 ml) balsamic vinegar
⅓ cup (80 ml) barbecue sauce
⅓ cup (60 g) brown sugar
2 garlic cloves, crushed
2 teaspoons smoked paprika
2 teaspoons chilli garlic sauce
1 teaspoon liquid smoke (optional)

Chilli lime

Juice of 2 limes
2 tablespoons olive oil
6–8 coriander (cilantro) sprigs, leaves picked and chopped
2 small chillies, finely diced
2 teaspoons ground cumin
2 teaspoons brown sugar
Large pinch of salt and pepper

Garlic tomato

⅓ cup (90 g) tomato paste (concentrated purée)
2 tablespoons olive oil (add more if marinade is too thick)
4–6 basil sprigs, leaves picked and chopped
2 small chillies, finely diced
2 garlic cloves, thinly sliced
Large pinch of salt and pepper

Beef, lamb and pork marinades

Suitable for steaks, chops, cutlets, fillets, kebabs and tofu steaks.

Add all of the marinade ingredients to a bowl and mix well. Pour the marinade over 1 kg (2 lb 4 oz) beef, lamb, pork or tofu steaks and marinate in the fridge for at least 1 hour, preferably overnight. (Tofu needs to be pressed to draw out the excess liquid before marinating. I love to marinate it overnight and then air fry it to make it extra crispy.)

Drain the marinated meat or tofu and cook it on a hot barbecue or chargrill pan until cooked through.

Oyster and soy

½ cup (125 ml) oyster sauce
⅓ cup (80 ml) soy sauce
2 tablespoons sesame oil
2 tablespoons grated ginger
4 garlic cloves, crushed
2 spring onions (scallions), finely diced
2 small red chillies, finely diced (optional)

Tip: For a vegetarian meal,
use mushroom oyster sauce.

Herb and lemon

½ cup (125 ml) olive oil
½ cup flat-leaf parsley leaves, finely chopped
½ cup coriander (cilantro) leaves, finely chopped
4 garlic cloves, crushed
Large pinch of salt and pepper
Lemon juice, to taste (add after cooking)

Red wine and sage

1 cup (250 ml) red wine
⅓ cup (80 ml) olive oil
12–14 sage leaves, chopped
6 garlic cloves, crushed
1 teaspoon salt
1 teaspoon freshly ground black pepper
Lemon juice, to taste

Rosemary and garlic

½ cup (125 ml) olive oil
6 rosemary sprigs, leaves picked and chopped
4 garlic cloves, sliced
Large pinch of salt and pepper
Lemon juice, to taste (add after cooking)

Beef, lamb and pork marinades

Greek
(see page 34)
Herb
and lemon
RECIPES PREVIOUS PAGE

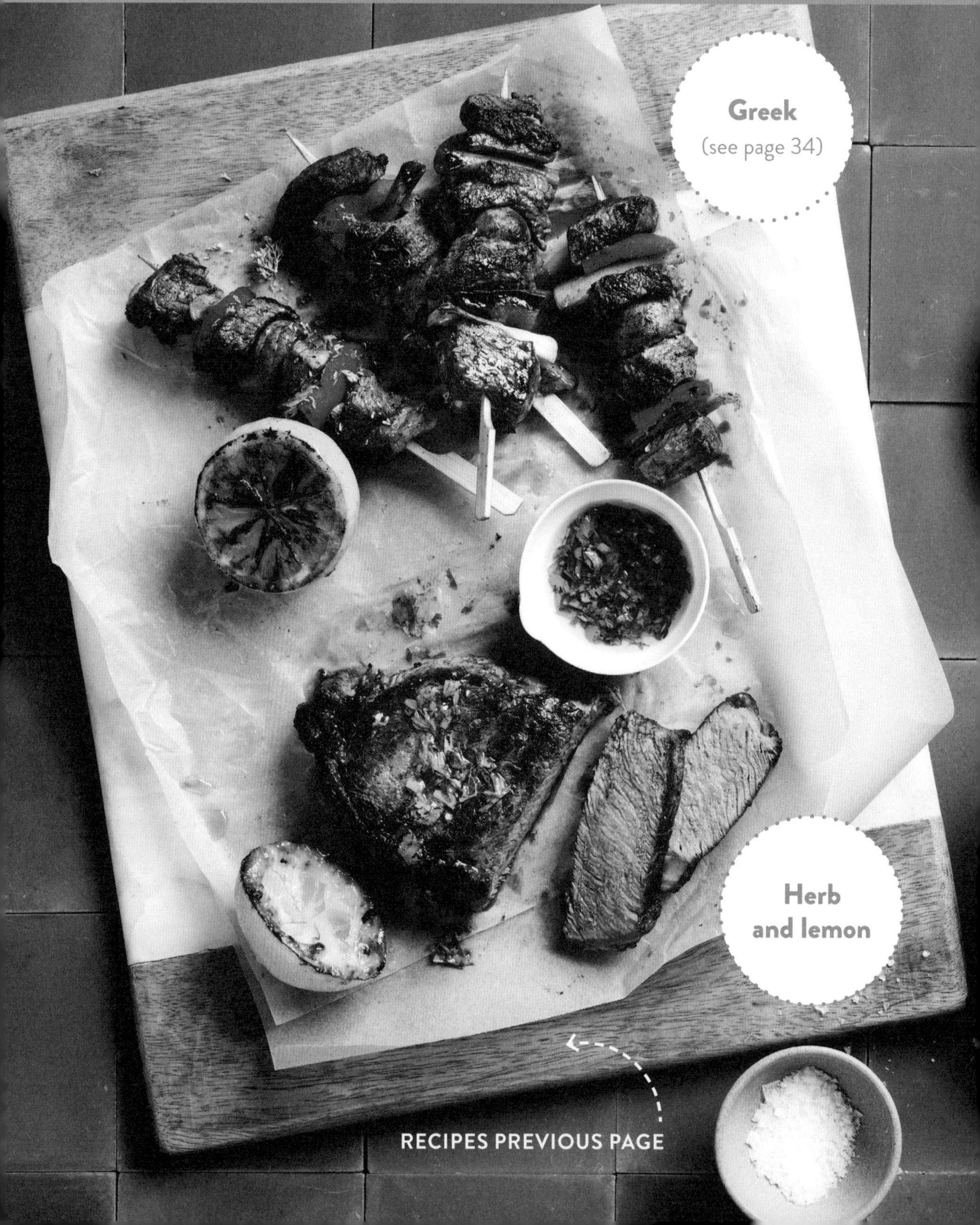

Oyster and soy tofu

Red wine and sage

Rosemary and garlic

Oyster and soy

Tomato
and lemon

Thai

Teriyaki
tempeh
(see page 28)

Fajita

Teriyaki
(see page 28)

Greek

RECIPES OVER PAGE

Fish and seafood marinades

Suitable for fish fillets or cutlets, whole fish (filleted), prawns, calamari rings, baby squid and tempeh.

Add all of the marinade ingredients to a bowl and mix well. Pour the marinade over 1 kg (2 lb 4 oz) fish, seafood or tempeh and marinate in the fridge for 1 hour. If you're using a whole fish, use a sharp knife to lightly score the top of the cleaned fish so the marinade penetrates beyond the skin, and ensure you marinate the inner cavity.

Drain the marinated fish, seafood or tempeh and cook it on a hot barbecue or chargrill pan until cooked through.

Greek

½ cup (125 ml) olive oil
10–12 basil leaves, sliced
4 garlic cloves, crushed
1 teaspoon sweet paprika
1 teaspoon dried oregano
Grated zest of 2 lemons
Lemon juice, to taste
Large pinch of salt and pepper

Fajita

2 teaspoons sweet paprika
2 teaspoons onion powder
2 teaspoons garlic powder
1 teaspoon dried oregano
½ teaspoon ground cumin
½ teaspoon cayenne pepper
Large pinch of salt and pepper

Thai

Juice of 2 limes
⅓ cup (80 ml) fish sauce
2 tablespoons caster (superfine) sugar
10 Thai basil leaves
6 kaffir lime leaves
2 small green chillies, sliced
2 coriander (cilantro) roots

Put all the ingredients in a blender and blend until combined.

Tomato and lemon

Juice of 1 lemon
10 cherry tomatoes, diced
½ red onion, diced
1 garlic clove, crushed
4–6 flat-leaf parsley sprigs, roughly chopped
Pinch of salt and pepper

The more colour in your meals, the better!

VEGGIES 4 WAYS

}

I love vegetables and I grew up eating them with
every meal. I'm passionate about getting people to try
something new – who knows, you might end up with a new bestie!
I've chosen some of the more common vegetables that people
may steer clear of because they think of them as being 'boring'
or just popped on the plate for colour, and given some easy
ideas for making them sing.

Mushrooms

Mushroom sauce

Heat 1 tablespoon olive oil in a small frying pan over medium–high heat. Add 10 thinly sliced button mushrooms and cook for 3 minutes, then add ½ small thinly sliced red onion and cook for another 2–3 minutes or until the mushrooms have softened and the liquid has evaporated. Stir in 200 ml (7 fl oz) thickened cream, ¼ cup (60 ml) chicken stock and 1 tablespoon chopped flat-leaf parsley. Season with salt and freshly ground black pepper. Bring to a low simmer, taste and adjust the seasoning if necessary. Cook for 15 minutes, allowing the sauce to slowly thicken. The longer you cook it, the thicker it will be. Serve the sauce over a juicy steak or some hot potato chips.

Serves 2–4

Garlic mushrooms

Preheat the oven to 180°C (350°F). Remove the stems from 2 portobello mushrooms and place each mushroom on a piece of foil large enough to wrap it up. Combine ¼ cup (60 ml) olive oil, 1 tablespoon chopped flat-leaf parsley, 2 crushed garlic cloves and 1 finely diced small red chilli. Brush the mixture over the mushrooms, completely covering them. Season with salt and freshly ground black pepper, then gather up the foil, ensuring no air can escape. Bake for 20 minutes.

Serves 2 as a side

Grated mushrooms (perfect for pasta!)

Carefully grate 5 firm button mushrooms, then slip them into dishes such as meatballs, bolognese and soup. You'll barely notice them, and there aren't any chunky bits (perfect for those of us who have partners or children who notice the slightest anomaly with their meals!). Make sure you use firm mushrooms, as soft or waterlogged ones are hard to grate.

Raw mushrooms (perfect in salad!)

Slice or dice 1 or 2 firm button mushrooms and add them to your salad – no cooking necessary! If the mushrooms are carrying a little soil, give them a brush or a quick wash first. Store-bought mushrooms are perfectly safe to eat raw. They can easily bulk up a meal while keeping the calories low.

Garlic
mushrooms

Raw
mushrooms

Grated
mushrooms

Mushroom sauce

RECIPES PREVIOUS PAGE

Broccoli

Lemony broccoli

Roasted chilli broccoli

Soy and garlic broccoli

Cheesy broccoli

RECIPES OVER PAGE

Broccoli

Lemony broccoli

Cut 1 broccoli head into florets and boil or steam for a maximum of 5 minutes – they should still have a little bit of a crunch. Drizzle the juice of 1 lemon and 1 tablespoon olive oil over the broccoli and season with salt and freshly ground black pepper.

Serves 3–4 as a side

Cheesy broccoli

Cut 1 broccoli head into florets and thinly slice the stems. Place in a heatproof bowl, cover with boiling water and leave for 2–3 minutes, then drain well. Heat 1 tablespoon olive oil in a small non-stick frying pan over medium heat. Cook the broccoli for 3–4 minutes or until tender but with a slight crunch, then add 1 sliced garlic clove and cook for 1 minute. Season with salt and freshly ground black pepper. Remove the broccoli from the pan and sprinkle with ¼ cup (25 g) grated parmesan or pecorino cheese.

Serves 3–4 as a side

Soy and garlic broccoli

Cut 1 broccoli head into florets and thinly slice the stems. Place in a heatproof bowl, cover with boiling water and leave for 2–3 minutes, then drain well. Heat 1 tablespoon sesame oil in a small non-stick frying pan over medium heat. Cook the broccoli for 3–4 minutes or until tender but with a slight crunch, then add 1 sliced garlic clove and cook for 1 minute. Stir in 1 tablespoon soy sauce and chilli flakes, to taste.

Serves 3–4 as a side

Roasted chilli broccoli

Preheat the oven to 180°C (350°F). Line a baking tray with baking paper. Cut 1 broccoli head into florets and place in a bowl. Add the juice of 1 lemon, 2–3 tablespoons grated parmesan cheese, 1–2 tablespoons olive oil and 1 finely diced small red chilli. Season with salt and freshly ground black pepper and toss until well combined, then tip the broccoli onto the baking tray. Roast for 15 minutes or until the broccoli florets are lightly golden.

Serves 3–4 as a side

Cauliflower

Cauliflower pizza base

Preheat the oven to 180°C (350°F). Line a baking tray with baking paper. Using a grater or food processor, finely grate or chop 1 cauliflower head into 'rice'. Steam the cauliflower in the microwave with a couple of tablespoons of water for 10 minutes. Cool slightly, then tip it onto a clean muslin cloth to draw out the excess water. Transfer the cauliflower to a bowl, add 2 tablespoons grated cheddar cheese, 1 crushed garlic clove, 1 egg, 1 teaspoon dried oregano, ¼ teaspoon chilli flakes and a pinch of salt and pepper and mix well. Shape the mixture into 1 large or 2 medium circles on the baking tray. Bake for 30 minutes or until golden, then add your favourite toppings and bake for 10 minutes.

Makes 1 large or 2 medium bases

Grated cauliflower (perfect for hiding veggies in a stir-fry!)

Coarsely grate ¼ cauliflower head. You can fry it in a little olive oil until soft or use it raw – slip it into dishes such as meatballs, bolognese and soup without a trace.

Roasted curried cauliflower

Preheat the oven to 180°C (350°F). Line a baking tray with baking paper. Cut ½ cauliflower head into florets and place it in a large bowl. Combine 2–3 tablespoons olive oil, 1 teaspoon curry powder, 1 teaspoon dried rosemary, ½ teaspoon chilli flakes, ¼ teaspoon ground turmeric and ½ teaspoon salt in another bowl, then pour the mixture over the cauliflower and toss to coat well. Tip the cauliflower onto the baking tray and roast for 45 minutes.

Serves 2–4 as a side

Roasted cheesy herb cauliflower

Preheat the oven to 180°C (350°F). Line a baking tray with baking paper. Cut ½ cauliflower head into florets and place it in a large bowl. Combine 2 tablespoons olive oil, 2 tablespoons grated parmesan or pecorino cheese, 2 tablespoons panko breadcrumbs, 1 tablespoon roughly chopped flat-leaf parsley, ½ teaspoon sweet paprika and a pinch of salt and pepper in another bowl, then pour the mixture over the cauliflower and toss to coat well. Tip the cauliflower onto the baking tray and roast for 45 minutes.

Serves 2–4 as a side

Roasted
cheesy herb
cauliflower

RECIPES PREVIOUS PAGE

Grated
cauliflower

Roasted curried cauliflower

Cauliflower pizza base

The LIGHT~

Meals that feel a little lighter, but are big on flavour

ER Side

1

THE
LIGHTER
SIDE

Roasted tomato bruschetta

Prep time: 10 minutes
Cook time: 10 minutes
Serves 2

---

2 cups (300 g) cherry
    tomatoes
2 garlic cloves, crushed
1 tablespoon extra virgin olive oil
4 thick slices wholemeal
    sourdough
¾ cup (185 g) ricotta cheese
15 g (½ oz) microgreens

OLIVE TAPENADE
½ cup (75 g) pitted kalamata
    olives
2 tablespoons baby capers,
    rinsed
2 tablespoons chives, chopped
1 handful flat-leaf parsley leaves
2 tablespoons extra virgin
    olive oil
1½ tablespoons lemon juice

Double the olive tapenade recipe and keep it in the fridge to add fast flavour to seafood, meats or a cheese board. Use gluten-free bread for a gluten-free version or soft cashew cheese instead of ricotta for a vegan option.

1   Preheat the oven to 220°C (425°F). Line a baking tray with baking paper. Place the tomatoes on the tray, toss with the crushed garlic and olive oil and season with salt and freshly ground black pepper. Add the sourdough slices to the tray and roast for 10 minutes.

2   Meanwhile, make the tapenade by blitzing the olives, capers, chives, parsley, olive oil and lemon juice in a food processor to form a chunky paste. Season with pepper.

3   Spread the toasted sourdough with the ricotta and top with the roasted tomatoes. Spoon the tapenade over the tomatoes and sprinkle with the microgreens. Serve immediately.

Carrot, cauliflower and corn fritters

Prep time: 15 minutes
Cook time: 25 minutes
Serves 4 (makes 8 fritters)

½ cup (90 g) potato starch
1 teaspoon baking powder
3 teaspoons ground coriander
2 teaspoons ground cumin
1 teaspoon ground ginger
4 egg whites
1 corncob, kernels removed
1 carrot, peeled and grated
1 cup (125 g) cauliflower florets,
 finely chopped
3 spring onions (scallions),
 chopped
1 handful flat-leaf parsley or
 coriander (cilantro) leaves,
 chopped
⅓ cup (80 ml) olive oil
3¾ cups (150 g) mixed
 salad leaves, to serve
150 g (5½ oz) soft goat's cheese
 or Persian feta, to serve

You can use different types of vegetables in these fritters, such as broccoli in place of cauliflower, zucchini (courgette) instead of carrot (squeeze out the excess liquid after grating) or frozen peas in place of the corn. This is a great recipe to freeze, and perfect for kids.

1 Combine the potato starch, baking powder and spices in a small bowl with some salt and freshly ground black pepper.

2 Using an electric mixer, whisk the egg whites until soft peaks form. Sift the dry ingredients over the egg whites and gently fold to combine. Add the vegetables and herbs and fold them through the batter.

3 Heat half of the olive oil in a large frying pan over medium–high heat. Drop ⅓ cup (80 ml) of the batter into the pan and spread it out a little. Repeat so that four fritters are cooking at a time. Cook for 5–6 minutes on each side or until the fritters are crisp and golden. Drain on paper towel and loosely cover with foil to keep warm while you cook the remaining fritters.

4 Stack the fritters and serve with salad leaves and goat's cheese.

Green pasta with pangrattato

Prep time: 15 minutes
Cook time: 20 minutes
Serves 4

2 tablespoons olive oil
1 brown onion, chopped
3 cups (120 g) chopped kale
¾ cup (100 g) frozen baby peas
4 garlic cloves, crushed
1 cup (250 ml) vegetable stock
500 g (1 lb 2 oz) pasta shells
1 avocado, halved
1 tablespoon lemon juice
1 bunch basil, leaves picked
200 g (7 oz) Danish feta
  cheese, crumbled

PANGRATTATO

1 tablespoon garlic-infused
  olive oil
½ cup (30 g) panko breadcrumbs
2 teaspoons finely grated
  lemon zest

You have to try this! It's simple, but so flavoursome. You could easily make it vegan by using vegan feta cheese. For a gluten-free meal, use gluten-free pasta and breadcrumbs.

1   Bring a large saucepan of salted water to the boil.

2   Meanwhile, heat the olive oil in a saucepan over medium–high heat. Cook the onion for a couple of minutes, then add the kale and cook for a few more minutes. Add the peas and garlic and cook for 2 minutes, then pour in the stock and simmer for 5 minutes. Remove from the heat.

3   Add the pasta to the boiling water and cook according to the packet instructions. Drain the pasta well, reserving ¼ cup (60 ml) of the water, and return to the pan.

4   Meanwhile, to make the pangrattato, heat the garlic oil in a frying pan over medium–high heat. Add the breadcrumbs and lemon zest and cook, stirring regularly, for a few minutes or until crisp and golden. Season with salt and freshly ground black pepper.

5   Pour the vegetable mixture into a blender and add the pasta water, avocado flesh, lemon juice and basil, reserving a few leaves for garnishing. Season with salt and pepper and blend until smooth.

6   Stir the sauce through the pasta. Serve topped with the feta, pangrattato and reserved basil leaves.

Pumpkin, carrot, ginger and coconut soup

Prep time: 15 minutes
Cook time: 35 minutes
Serves 4–6

1 kg (2 lb 4 oz) butternut
  pumpkin (squash)
½ bunch coriander (cilantro)
1 tablespoon olive oil
2 brown onions, chopped
3 carrots, peeled and chopped
1½ tablespoons finely grated
  ginger
3 garlic cloves, crushed
1½ teaspoons curry powder
4 kaffir lime leaves, bruised
4 cups (1 litre) vegetable stock
1 cup (250 ml) coconut milk,
  plus extra to serve

CHILLI PEPITAS
½ cup (75 g) pepitas
  (pumpkin seeds)
2 teaspoons olive oil
2 teaspoons onion powder
½ teaspoon chilli powder

This soup is seriously delicious, especially in winter when you just want to cuddle up and be warm. The chilli pepitas make a great snack and add crunch to salads. Double the recipe, cool and store in an airtight container for up to 2 weeks.

1 Preheat the oven to 160°C (315°F). Line a baking tray with baking paper.

2 Peel, seed and chop the pumpkin. Wash and chop the coriander roots and stems. Set the leaves aside.

3 Combine the olive oil, onion and carrot in a stockpot and place over medium–high heat. Cook for 5 minutes or until the vegetables are beginning to colour. Add the coriander roots and stems, ginger, garlic and curry powder and cook for a couple of minutes. Add the pumpkin, lime leaves, stock and coconut milk and season with salt and freshly ground black pepper. Bring to the boil, reduce the heat to medium–low and simmer for 25 minutes or until the vegetables are soft.

4 Meanwhile, prepare the chilli pepitas. Combine the pepitas, olive oil, onion powder, chilli powder and some salt in a small bowl. Tumble the pepitas onto the baking tray in a single layer and roast for 10–12 minutes or until golden, stirring halfway through cooking. Keep an eye on them as they can burn easily.

5 Remove and discard the lime leaves and purée the soup with a stick blender.

6 Ladle the soup into bowls. Drizzle with a little extra coconut milk and sprinkle with the chilli pepitas, coriander leaves and some freshly ground black pepper.

Roasted panzanella

Prep time: 10 minutes
Cook time: 15 minutes
Serves 2

---

150 g (5½ oz) wholemeal
    sourdough
200 g (7 oz) Greek feta cheese
500 g (1 lb 2 oz) baby heirloom
    tomatoes
1 red onion, cut into thin
    wedges
¼ cup (60 ml) garlic-infused
    olive oil
1½ tablespoons red wine vinegar
1 bunch basil, leaves picked

This salad is wonderful as a light meal for 2 people or as a side dish for 4 people with seafood or meat. It's one of my favourites when I have guests coming for dinner in summer because the tomatoes are so fresh and full of flavour.

1   Preheat the oven to 220°C (425°F). Line a baking tray with baking paper.

2   Break the sourdough and feta into bite-sized pieces and add them to a large bowl with the tomatoes and onion wedges. Pour in the garlic oil and toss well to combine. Season with salt and freshly ground black pepper.

3   Tumble the tomato mixture onto the baking tray and roast for 15 minutes or until the tomatoes are soft and the bread is golden.

4   Leave the mixture to cool slightly before returning it to the large bowl with the roasting juices. Gently toss the vinegar and basil through the salad, then serve.

Spanakorizo with beans

Prep time: 10 minutes
Cook time: 25 minutes
Serves 4

---

2 tablespoons olive oil
1 brown onion, finely diced
2 garlic cloves, crushed
1 small chilli, finely diced
500 g (1 lb 2 oz) baby spinach
¼ cup (60 g) tomato paste
   (concentrated purée)
⅔ cup (135 g) long-grain rice,
   rinsed
2½ cups (625 ml) chicken stock
400 g (14 oz) tin cannellini
   beans, rinsed and drained

Cannellini beans are a high-protein option for this dish, but you could also use shredded chicken, meatballs or chickpeas. It's also lovely topped with a little crumbled feta cheese.

1   Heat the olive oil in a deep saucepan over medium heat. Cook the onion, garlic and chilli for 3–4 minutes or until the onion is translucent.

2   Add the spinach and tomato paste and cook for 2–3 minutes or until the spinach has wilted.

3   Stir in the rice, stock and cannellini beans and season with salt and freshly ground black pepper. Cover and simmer for 15 minutes.

4   Serve immediately, sprinkled with freshly ground black pepper.

Summer prawn salad

Prep time: 25 minutes
Cook time: 5 minutes
Serves 2

¼ cup (60 ml) reduced-fat
    coconut milk
2 tablespoons lime juice
1½ tablespoons smooth peanut
    butter
1½ tablespoons hoisin sauce
1 garlic clove, crushed
2 teaspoons brown sugar
2 teaspoons sriracha hot chilli
    sauce
100 g (3½ oz) dried rice stick
    noodles
1 carrot, peeled into ribbons
12 cooked prawns, peeled and
    deveined, tails on
120 g (4¼ oz) snow peas
    (mange tout), sliced
2 spring onions (scallions),
    sliced
1 cup (115 g) bean sprouts
1 handful mint leaves
¼ cup (35 g) crushed peanuts

This salad is also lovely with shredded barbecue chicken instead of the prawns. For a vegan version, use firm tofu or a vegan chicken substitute.

1   Combine the coconut milk, lime juice, peanut butter, hoisin sauce, garlic, brown sugar and sriracha in a small saucepan. Stir over medium heat for a couple of minutes to dissolve the sugar. Remove from the heat and set aside to cool.

2   Place the noodles in a large heatproof bowl and cover with boiling water. Leave to soak for 8–10 minutes or until tender, then drain and rinse under cold water.

3   Place the noodles and carrot ribbons in a large bowl and toss with half the dressing. Divide the noodles and carrot between two bowls and top with the prawns, snow peas, spring onion, bean sprouts, mint and peanuts. Serve with the remaining dressing on the side.

Tip: Use a vegetable peeler to peel the carrot into ribbons.

Quick chicken empanadas

Prep time: 25 minutes
Cook time: 30 minutes
Makes 8

300 g (10½ oz) chicken mince
100 g (3½ oz) chorizo, finely
    chopped
2 tablespoons tomato paste
    (concentrated purée)
120 g (4¼ oz) marinated red
    capsicum (pepper), finely
    chopped (see page 184)
150 g (5½ oz) sweet potato,
    peeled and grated
4 spring onions (scallions),
    chopped
2 teaspoons sweet paprika
2 tablespoons oregano leaves
4 sheets shortcrust pastry,
    thawed
1 egg, whisked

Using store-bought shortcrust pastry and a filling that doesn't require precooking makes these much faster to make than traditional empanadas. If you can't pinch and fold the pastry over in the traditional way, you can simply press the edges with a fork to seal it well.

1   Preheat the oven to 200°C (400°F). Line a baking tray with baking paper.

2   Mix all the ingredients except the pastry and egg in a large bowl (the best way to do this is with clean hands). Season with salt and freshly ground black pepper.

3   Cut two 14 cm (5½ inch) circles from each pastry sheet so that you have eight circles. Divide the filling mixture evenly among the centre of the pastry rounds. Fold up the sides and press the pastry together to seal. Pinch the edge of the pastry and fold over, repeating all the way along the edge to seal. Place the empanadas on the baking tray.

4   Brush both sides of the pastry with the egg and bake the empanadas for about 30 minutes or until they are golden and cooked through.

Huevos rancheros soup

Prep time: 15 minutes
Cook time: 25 minutes
Serves 4

2 tablespoons olive oil
1 large brown onion, chopped
200 g (7 oz) marinated red
    capsicum (pepper), chopped
    (see page 184)
4 garlic cloves, crushed
1 jalapeño chilli, finely chopped
3 teaspoons ground coriander
2 teaspoons ground cumin
1½ teaspoons sweet paprika
3 cups (750 ml) vegetable
    stock
1½ cups (375 ml) tomato
    passata (puréed tomatoes)
3 x 400 g (14 oz) tins red
    kidney beans, rinsed and
    drained
1 tablespoon white vinegar
4 eggs
1 tomato, seeds removed,
    chopped
1 handful coriander (cilantro)
    leaves
Low-fat sour cream, to serve
Chopped spring onions
    (scallions), to serve

CRUNCHY TORTILLAS
4 mini tortillas
Olive oil spray
Sea salt flakes, for sprinkling
Sweet paprika, for sprinkling

You've probably never come across huevos rancheros as a soup.
But it's incredible, I promise! You can serve it with store-bought
tortilla chips instead of making your own if you want to take
a shortcut.

1   Preheat the oven to 200°C (400°F). Line a baking tray with
    baking paper.

2   Heat the olive oil in a large saucepan over medium–high heat
    and cook the onion for a few minutes. Stir in the capsicum,
    garlic, chilli, ground coriander, cumin and paprika and cook
    for another couple of minutes. Pour in the stock, passata and
    two-thirds of the kidney beans and simmer for 15 minutes.

3   Meanwhile, place the tortillas on the baking tray, spray with
    olive oil and sprinkle with sea salt and a little paprika. Bake for
    5 minutes, then turn and cook for 3–5 minutes or until golden.
    Set aside to cool and crisp up.

4   Bring a saucepan of water to the boil. Add the vinegar and
    reduce the heat to low. Stir the water to create a whirlpool,
    then add the eggs, one at a time, and poach for 2½ minutes
    or until the whites are set but the yolks are still runny (or until
    cooked to your liking). Remove with a slotted spoon and drain
    on paper towel.

5   Purée the soup using a stick blender, then stir in the remaining
    kidney beans and cook until heated through.

6   Ladle the soup into bowls and top each with an egg, tomato,
    coriander leaves, sour cream, spring onion and freshly ground
    black pepper. Serve with the crunchy tortillas.

Roasted cauliflower, carrot and feta freekeh salad

Prep time: 15 minutes
Cook time: 30 minutes
Serves 2

⅔ cup (130 g) freekeh
¼ cup (60 ml) extra virgin
    olive oil
1½ tablespoons maple syrup
3 garlic cloves, crushed
1½ teaspoons ground cumin
½ teaspoon ground turmeric
¼ teaspoon cayenne pepper
¼ cauliflower, cut into small
    florets
1 bunch Dutch carrots, halved
    lengthways
1 small red onion, cut
    into wedges
⅓ cup (50 g) pine nuts
1½ tablespoons apple cider
    vinegar
2 teaspoons dijon mustard
½ bunch chives, chopped
1¼ cups (60 g) baby spinach
½ bunch mint leaves, chopped
100 g (3½ oz) Persian feta
    cheese

I seriously love roasted cauliflower! Roasting brings out a much better flavour than boiling or steaming. Substitute vegan feta for a vegan meal, and use brown rice instead of freekeh for a gluten-free version.

1   Preheat the oven to 180°C (350°F). Line a baking tray with baking paper.

2   Bring a saucepan of salted water to the boil. Add the freekeh and cook for 30 minutes or until al dente. Drain and rinse under cold water to cool; drain well and set aside.

3   Meanwhile, combine half of the olive oil with the maple syrup, garlic, spices and some salt and freshly ground black pepper in a large bowl. Add the cauliflower, carrots and onion and toss to coat.

4   Tumble the vegetables onto the tray and roast for 20 minutes. Scatter the pine nuts over the vegetables and cook for another 5 minutes or until the vegetables are just tender.

5   Combine the vinegar, mustard, chives and remaining olive oil in a large bowl. Add the freekeh, spinach and mint and toss to combine. Season with salt and pepper.

6   Divide the freekeh between serving plates and add the roasted vegetables and pine nuts. Crumble the feta over the salad, sprinkle with freshly ground black pepper and serve.

Hoisin salmon lettuce wraps

Prep time: 10 minutes,
  plus marinating
Cook time: 15 minutes
Serves 4

⅓ cup (80 ml) hoisin sauce

¼ cup (60 ml) soy sauce

1 teaspoon sesame oil

3 garlic cloves, crushed

3 teaspoons grated ginger

3 x 180 g (6 oz) skinless salmon
  fillets

3 teaspoons sesame seeds

12 iceberg lettuce cups

2 Lebanese (short) cucumbers,
  julienned

3 spring onions (scallions),
  julienned

1 handful coriander (cilantro),
  to serve

You can add cooked rice or some avocado slices to make this more substantial. Adding simple extras like this can really bulk out a meal and keep you feeling fuller for longer.

1   Preheat the oven to 180°C (350°F). Line a baking tray with baking paper.

2   Combine the hoisin sauce, soy sauce, sesame oil, garlic and ginger in a bowl. Add the salmon fillets and turn to coat well. Set aside to marinate for 15 minutes (or up to an hour in the fridge, if you have time).

3   Meanwhile, pour the sesame seeds onto the baking tray and bake for 5 minutes or until golden. Pour the toasted seeds into a small bowl. Set aside.

4   Place the salmon on the lined tray and pour the remaining marinade over the top. Bake for about 10 minutes or until cooked to your liking. Remove from the oven and set aside to rest for a few minutes.

5   Flake the salmon into large chunks and drizzle the cooking juices over the top. Fill the lettuce cups with the salmon, cucumber and spring onion and top with the coriander and toasted sesame seeds.

Garlic and herb mushrooms on lemon mascarpone toast

Prep time: 15 minutes
Cook time: 10 minutes
Serves 2

---

300 g (10½ oz) Swiss brown
   mushrooms
150 g (5½ oz) shiitake
   mushrooms
150 g (5½ oz) oyster mushrooms
1½ tablespoons (30 g) butter
1 tablespoon olive oil
2 tablespoons oregano leaves
1½ tablespoons thyme leaves
3 garlic cloves, crushed
2 tablespoons chopped chives
1 handful flat-leaf parsley
   leaves, chopped
⅔ cup (165 g) mascarpone
   cheese
1 tablespoon lemon juice
1 teaspoon grated lemon zest
4 thick slices rye sourdough or
   bread of choice, toasted

This recipe is going to be become your new favourite, I just know it! If you can't find the shiitake mushrooms, use regular mushrooms instead.

1 Halve or quarter the Swiss brown mushrooms, depending on their size. Slice the shiitake mushrooms and tear the oyster mushrooms in half.

2 Heat the butter and the olive oil in a large frying pan over medium–high heat. Cook the Swiss brown and shiitake mushrooms, oregano and thyme, stirring occasionally, for 5 minutes. Add the oyster mushrooms and garlic and cook for a few more minutes. Remove from the heat, stir in the chives and parsley and season with salt and freshly ground black pepper.

3 While the mushrooms are cooking, combine the mascarpone, lemon juice and lemon zest and season with salt and pepper.

4 Spread the lemon mascarpone over the toasted sourdough and top with the mushrooms. Serve immediately.

Quick Buffalo chicken and corn quesadillas

Prep time: 10 minutes
Cook time: 10 minutes
Serves 2

¼ cup (60 g) low-fat cream cheese, softened
1½ tablespoons hot sauce
1 cup (150 g) shredded barbecue chicken
½ cup (100 g) fresh corn kernels
2 spring onions (scallions), chopped
1 handful coriander (cilantro) leaves, chopped
¾ cup (105 g) grated mozzarella cheese
4 wholegrain tortillas
Lime wedges, to serve

A great trick for turning your quesadillas is to hold a plate on top of the pan and flip the quesadilla onto it, then slide it back into the pan to cook the other side. You can make this a gluten-free meal by using gluten-free tortillas.

1 Combine the cream cheese and hot sauce in a bowl. Stir in the chicken, corn, spring onion, coriander and mozzarella. Season with salt and freshly ground black pepper.

2 Spread the chicken mixture over two tortillas and top with the remaining tortillas. Cook in a large non-stick frying pan or chargrill pan over medium heat for 4–5 minutes on each side or until the tortillas are crisp and the filling is hot.

3 Cut the quesadillas into quarters and serve with lime wedges.

Quick spanakopita pies

Prep time: 15 minutes
Cook time: 20 minutes
Makes 6

6 sheets filo pastry
50 g (1¾ oz) butter, melted
250 g (9 oz) frozen chopped
    spinach, thawed
3 spring onions (scallions),
    chopped
2 tablespoons chopped dill
100 g (3½ oz) Greek feta
    cheese, crumbled
6 eggs, chilled

You can thank Yiayia Itsines for these pies! She loves to make them for our family gatherings, and when they're sitting on the table, we all know how good they're going to be. The pies are best served warm, and can be frozen and reheated in the oven. It's important to use the eggs straight from the fridge so they don't overcook by the time the pastry is ready.

1   Preheat the oven to 180°C (350°F).

2   Lightly brush a sheet of filo with melted butter and top with another sheet. Brush with more butter and repeat with the remaining pastry. Brush the final layer with butter and cut the pastry stack into six even pieces. Press the pastry into six ½ cup (125 ml) capacity muffin holes with the buttered sides facing down.

3   Squeeze the thawed spinach to remove the excess liquid, then put it in a bowl and stir in the spring onion, dill and feta. Season with salt and freshly ground black pepper. Spoon the spinach mixture into the pastry cups.

4   Make a well in the centre of the spinach mixture in each pastry cup, pushing it up the sides of the pastry, and crack an egg into the middle. Bake for 20 minutes or until the pastry is golden and the egg yolks are done to your liking. Serve sprinkled with freshly ground black pepper.

Eggplant, chickpea and shaved haloumi salad

Prep time: 15 minutes
Cook time: 50 minutes
Serves 2

⅓ cup (50 g) blanched almonds
⅔ cup (110 g) tinned chickpeas, rinsed and drained
2 tablespoons garlic-infused olive oil
3 Lebanese eggplants (aubergines), halved
¼ cup (40 g) sun-dried tomatoes
¼ cup (60 ml) extra virgin olive oil
1 garlic clove, crushed
3 cups (135 g) baby rocket (arugula) leaves
75 g (2½ oz) haloumi, shaved (see Tip)
Lemon wedges, to serve

Crispy chickpeas make a great snack. Make them as I've done here or mix together different spices such as paprika, cumin, onion powder, garlic powder and ground coriander to toss them in when they're fresh out of the oven. They'll get super crispy and cook faster if you cook them in an air fryer.

1 Preheat the oven to 200°C (400°F). Line two baking trays with baking paper. Spread the almonds over one tray and roast for 5–8 minutes or until lightly golden. Set aside to cool slightly.

2 Pat the chickpeas dry with paper towel, then tumble them onto the other tray and coat with half of the garlic oil and some salt. Push the chickpeas to one side of the tray and add the eggplant. Drizzle the remaining garlic oil over the eggplant and season with salt and freshly ground black pepper. Roast for 40 minutes or until the eggplant is soft in the middle and the chickpeas are crisp. Stir the chickpeas occasionally while they're cooking so they cook evenly.

3 Meanwhile, tip the cooled almonds, sun-dried tomatoes, extra virgin olive oil, garlic and ⅓ cup (80 ml) water into a blender and blitz to a chunky paste. Season with salt and pepper.

4 Spread the almond sauce onto serving plates and layer the rocket, eggplant, chickpeas and haloumi on top. Serve with lemon wedges.

Tip: Use a vegetable peeler to shave the haloumi.

Roasted sweet potato and broccoli frittata

Prep time: 15 minutes
Cook time: 50 minutes
Serves 6

---

250 g (9 oz) sweet potato,
   peeled and cut into
   small pieces
1 red onion, cut into thin wedges
2½ cups (150 g) small broccoli
   florets
Olive oil spray
2 tablespoons thyme leaves
12 eggs
¾ cup (185 ml) milk
150 g (5½ oz) soft goat's cheese

This frittata is great either hot or cold. You can freeze it in single slices, ready to add to a lunchbox. For a silkier frittata, replace ½ cup (125 ml) of the milk with single (pure) cream.

1   Preheat the oven to 180°C (350°F). Line a baking tray and a 25 cm (10 inch) round ovenproof dish with baking paper.

2   Spread the sweet potato, onion and broccoli over the tray. Spray with olive oil, sprinkle with the thyme and season with salt and freshly ground black pepper. Roast for 25 minutes or until the sweet potato is just tender.

3   Whisk the eggs and milk together and season with salt and pepper. Pour the mixture into the lined dish. Add the roasted vegetables, dividing them evenly throughout the egg mixture, and dot with the goat's cheese. Bake for 20–25 minutes or until the mixture is just set.

Tip: To easily line a round dish, scrunch up a sheet of baking paper, then flatten it out and press it into the dish.

Turkey and vegetable sausage rolls

Prep time: 25 minutes
Cook time: 30 minutes
Makes 16

500 g (1 lb 2 oz) turkey mince
1 zucchini (courgette), grated
1 carrot, peeled and grated
⅔ cup (80 g) dried
    breadcrumbs
⅓ cup (45 g) bottled
    caramelised onion
1 tablespoon thyme leaves
2 sheets reduced-fat puff
    pastry, thawed
1 egg, whisked
1 teaspoon poppy seeds

TOMATO RELISH
3 tomatoes
1 tablespoon olive oil
2 garlic cloves, crushed
¼ cup (35 g) bottled
    caramelised onion
1 tablespoon oregano leaves
¼ teaspoon cayenne pepper

If you're making these for kids who won't eat green vegetables, you can peel the zucchini before grating it and omit the thyme. The uncooked sausage rolls freeze well, so when you're super busy you can throw them straight in the oven for a quick meal.

1   Preheat the oven to 200°C (400°F). Line a baking tray with baking paper.

2   Combine the turkey mince, zucchini, carrot, breadcrumbs, caramelised onion and thyme in a large bowl. Season with salt and freshly ground black pepper.

3   Cut the pastry sheets in half. Lay a quarter of the turkey and vegetable mixture along the long side of a piece of pastry, moulding it into a sausage shape. Brush the other edge with egg, then tightly roll up to encase the filling and place on the baking tray, seam side down. Repeat with the remaining pastry and filling. Brush the sausage rolls with egg and sprinkle with the poppy seeds. Use a sharp knife to cut halfway through the top of each roll to make four even pieces – this helps the rolls cook evenly and also makes it easy to break them into portions later. Bake for 30 minutes or until puffed and golden.

4   Meanwhile, make the tomato relish. Cut a cross in the base of each tomato with a small, sharp knife and place in a bowl of boiling water for 20 seconds. Remove the tomatoes from the water and peel away the skin. Halve the tomatoes, scoop out the seeds and chop the flesh.

5   Heat the olive oil in a small saucepan over medium heat. Cook the garlic for 1 minute, then add the chopped tomato, caramelised onion, oregano, cayenne pepper and some salt. Gently simmer, stirring occasionally, for 10–15 minutes or until thickened.

6   Serve the sausage rolls with the warm tomato relish.

Tip: You can use chicken mince in place of the turkey mince.

Chicken and whipped feta salad

Prep time: 20 minutes
Cook time: 20 minutes
Serves 2

1 large boneless, skinless
   chicken breast
Juice of 1 lemon
1 garlic clove, crushed
½ teaspoon sweet paprika
Dried oregano, for sprinkling
Olive oil, for cooking and
   drizzling
1 Lebanese (short) cucumber,
   cut into chunks
6 cherry tomatoes, quartered
6 kalamata olives, halved
   and pitted
½ red capsicum (pepper),
   cut into small strips
½ red onion, thinly sliced

WHIPPED FETA
½ cup (65 g) crumbled feta
   cheese
½ cup (120 g) cream cheese
Grated zest and juice of
   ½ lemon
1 tablespoon chopped oregano
1 garlic clove

Whipping feta with cream cheese is super delicious and a perfect way to make the feta into a smooth sauce rather than a crumbly topping. Browning the chicken breast in a pan and then finishing it off in the oven helps prevent it from drying out.

1 Preheat the oven to 180°C (350°F). Line a baking tray with baking paper.

2 Put the chicken in a bowl with half the lemon juice, the garlic, paprika, dried oregano and some salt and freshly ground black pepper. Toss to completely coat the chicken.

3 Drizzle a small non-stick frying pan with olive oil and place over medium–high heat. Lightly brown the chicken breast on all sides. Transfer the chicken to the baking tray and bake for 15 minutes or until completely cooked through. Cool slightly, then slice the chicken.

4 While the chicken is cooking, prepare the whipped feta. Combine the crumbled feta, cream cheese, lemon zest, lemon juice, chopped oregano and garlic in a small blender and blend until smooth.

5 Combine the cucumber, cherry tomatoes, olives, capsicum and red onion in a bowl. Drizzle with olive oil and the remaining lemon juice and sprinkle with salt.

6 Spread a large spoonful of the whipped feta over each serving plate and drizzle with a little olive oil. Add the salad and top with the chicken slices.

Crispy fish tacos with sweet chilli avocado salsa

Prep time: 15 minutes
Cook time: 15 minutes
Serves 4

---

600 g (1 lb 5 oz) firm white
  skinless fish fillets, such as
  snapper
½ cup (110 g) rice flour
1 teaspoon ground turmeric
2 teaspoons onion powder
Ground white pepper, to taste
Peanut oil, for frying
2 egg whites
8–10 butter lettuce leaves
8–10 mini tortillas

SWEET CHILLI AVOCADO SALSA

1½ tablespoons sweet chilli
  sauce
2 tablespoons lime juice
1–2 avocados, diced
1 Lebanese (short) cucumber,
  quartered lengthways, sliced
2 spring onions (scallions),
  chopped
1 handful coriander (cilantro),
  chopped

Use gluten-free tortillas for a gluten-free version. You can replace the fish with firm tofu for a vegetarian meal. I love tofu cooked in the air fryer – it has such a good crunch!

1 To make the salsa, stir the sweet chilli sauce and lime juice together in a bowl. Add the avocado, cucumber, spring onion and coriander and toss to coat. Season with salt and freshly ground black pepper. Set aside while you prepare the fish.

2 Cut the fish into thick strips.

3 Combine the rice flour, turmeric, onion powder, white pepper and a little salt in a large bowl.

4 Pour enough peanut oil into a large frying pan to come about 1 cm (½ inch) up the side of the pan and place the pan over medium–high heat.

5 Whisk the egg whites in a bowl until foamy. Add half of the fish and toss to coat, then dredge the fish pieces in the rice flour mixture. Cook the fish for a few minutes until crisp and cooked through. Drain on paper towel. Repeat with the remaining fish pieces.

6 Lay a lettuce leaf on each tortilla and top with the crispy fish and the salsa. Serve immediately.

Roasted kipfler potato, bean and asparagus salad

Prep time: 20 minutes
Cook time: 30 minutes
Serves 2

---

400 g (14 oz) kipfler (fingerling)
    potatoes
Olive oil spray
250 g (9 oz) green beans
1 bunch (about 150 g) asparagus
½ cup (60 g) pitted green olives
1 tablespoon white vinegar
4 eggs, chilled
Flat-leaf parsley leaves, to serve
Basil leaves, to serve

SALSA VERDE
1 handful flat-leaf parsley leaves
1 handful basil leaves
¼ cup chopped chives
2 tablespoons baby capers,
    rinsed
2 tablespoons lemon juice
1 tablespoon dijon mustard
⅓ cup (80 ml) extra virgin
    olive oil

Potato salad, but beautiful? Yes, please! I love a super-simple, quick-and-easy side dish with dinner and this is a really fresh option to have in summer. It's also a great dish to take along to a barbecue.

1 Preheat the oven to 200°C (400°F). Line a baking tray with baking paper.

2 Scrub the potatoes, cut them in half lengthways and place them on the tray. Spray with olive oil and roast for 15 minutes. Add the beans, asparagus and olives to the tray. Spray with a little more oil, season with salt and freshly ground black pepper and roast for a further 15 minutes.

3 Meanwhile, make the salsa verde. Blitz the parsley, basil, chives, capers, lemon juice and mustard in a food processor until roughly chopped. With the motor running, slowly pour in the olive oil. Season with salt and pepper.

4 Add the vinegar to a small saucepan of water and bring to the boil. Cook the eggs for 7½ minutes for soft-boiled eggs or until cooked to your liking. Pour off the boiling water and fill the pan with cold water. Set aside for 1 minute, or until the eggs are cool enough to peel.

5 Arrange the vegetables on a serving plate. Halve the eggs and place them on top of the vegetables. Drizzle the salsa verde over the salad and add some freshly ground black pepper. Finish with some parsley and basil leaves.

Tip: The vinegar in the water helps to set the whites if the shells crack, and also assists peeling.

Smoked salmon and avocado quinoa bowl

Prep time: 10 minutes
Cook time: 20 minutes
Serves 2

½ cup (100 g) tricolour quinoa
Large pinch of salt
2 tablespoons tamari or
    soy sauce
1½ tablespoons mirin
1 tablespoon lemon juice
2 teaspoons honey
1 bird's eye chilli, chopped
150 g (5½ oz) smoked salmon
    slices
1 avocado, chopped
1 Lebanese (short) cucumber,
    chopped
½ bunch (about 50 g)
    watercress, roughly chopped
2 tablespoons furikake
    seasoning (see Tip)

I love a quick-and-easy salad bowl for lunch. You can replace the smoked salmon with sashimi-grade tuna or salmon, or even barbecue chicken. Use firm tofu or a vegan chicken substitute for a vegan version.

1   Put the quinoa in a fine sieve and rinse under cold water until the water runs clear. Transfer the quinoa to a small saucepan with the salt and 1 cup (250 ml) water and bring to the boil over high heat. Reduce the heat to low, cover and cook for 15 minutes or until the water is absorbed and the quinoa is tender. Remove from the heat and fluff with a fork.

2   While the quinoa is cooking, combine the tamari, mirin, lemon juice, honey and chilli in a small bowl. Stir until the honey has dissolved.

3   Stir half of the dressing through the quinoa and spoon it into serving bowls. Arrange the smoked salmon, avocado, cucumber and watercress on top. Sprinkle the furikake and remaining dressing over the top.

Tip: You can replace the furikake seasoning with toasted sesame seeds or nori sprinkles.

Eggplant and potato bake

Prep time: 15 minutes,
  plus 30 minutes draining
Cook time: 1½ hours
Serves 4

---

2 large eggplants (aubergines)
1–2 tablespoons salt
Olive oil, for cooking
200 g (7 oz) potatoes,
  thinly sliced
1 red onion, cut into thick strips
2 garlic cloves, crushed
1 tablespoon tomato paste
  (concentrated purée)
½ cup (125 ml) bottled
  napoletana pasta sauce
⅓ cup (80 ml) chicken stock
1 tablespoon chopped flat-leaf
  parsley, plus extra to serve

When eggplants are in season, buy away! They're great to bulk up a meal while keeping the cost low. This can be served on its own, or with some rice for a larger meal.

1 Halve the eggplants lengthways, then cut them into thick slices and place in a colander sitting over a bowl. Sprinkle the salt over the eggplant, covering it completely. Leave to drain for 30 minutes to extract the excess liquid and bitterness. Pat the eggplant dry with paper towel.

2 Preheat the oven to 180°C (350°F).

3 Heat a splash of olive oil in a non-stick frying pan over medium heat. Fry the eggplant slices in batches until lightly golden brown on both sides. Transfer to a large bowl.

4 Heat another splash of olive oil, add the potato slices and season with salt and freshly ground black pepper. Cook for 2–3 minutes on each side or until lightly golden brown. Remove from the pan and set aside with the eggplant.

5 Add the onion and garlic to the pan and cook, stirring, for 3 minutes. Tip the mixture into the bowl with the eggplant and potato, add the tomato paste and season with salt and pepper. Add the pasta sauce and stock and mix well.

6 Pour the mixture into an ovenproof dish, sprinkle with the parsley and drizzle with a little olive oil. Cover with foil and bake for 1 hour.

7 Serve hot, sprinkled with extra chopped parsley.

Chicken and herb salad

Prep time: 15 minutes
Cook time: 10 minutes
Serves 2

1½ tablespoons olive oil
3 garlic cloves, crushed
1½ teaspoons ground cumin
1½ teaspoons smoked paprika
½ teaspoon ground cinnamon
400 g (14 oz) skinless, boneless
 chicken thighs
200 g (7 oz) mini roma
 tomatoes, halved
1 bunch flat-leaf parsley, leaves
 roughly chopped
½ bunch mint, leaves roughly
 chopped
2 spring onions (scallions),
 chopped
¼ cup (30 g) hemp seeds
Lemon wedges, to serve

DRESSING
¼ cup (60 ml) lemon juice
2 tablespoons tahini
2 tablespoons extra virgin
 olive oil
2 teaspoons honey
1 garlic clove, crushed

Herb-based salads are great because they're packed with fresh flavour. This is an easy salad that you can meal prep across the week. Use shredded barbecue chicken for a super-quick, no-cook meal.

1 Combine the olive oil, garlic, cumin, paprika and cinnamon in a bowl and season with salt and freshly ground black pepper. Add the chicken and turn to coat well.

2 Heat a chargrill or frying pan over medium–high heat. Cook the chicken, turning once, for 6–8 minutes or until cooked through. Set aside to rest before slicing.

3 Meanwhile, for the dressing, whisk the lemon juice, tahini, extra virgin olive oil, honey, garlic and 1 tablespoon water in a small bowl. Season with salt and pepper.

4 Toss the tomatoes, parsley, mint, spring onion, hemp seeds and half the dressing in a large bowl and season to taste. Divide the salad among serving plates, top with the sliced chicken and drizzle with the remaining dressing. Serve with lemon wedges.

Stuffed zucchini and eggplant

Prep time: 30 minutes
Cook time: 1¼ hours
Serves 4

---

4 small zucchini (courgettes)
4 small eggplants (aubergines)
¼ cup (60 ml) olive oil
1 brown onion, finely diced
2 garlic cloves, crushed
1 small red chilli, thinly sliced
½ cup firmly packed (25 g)
   mint leaves, finely chopped
½ cup firmly packed (25 g)
   flat-leaf parsley leaves,
   finely chopped
250 g (9 oz) lean beef mince
2 x 400 g (14 oz) tins crushed
   tomatoes
2 tablespoons tomato paste
   (concentrated purée)
1 tablespoon dried oregano
⅔ cup (135 g) long-grain rice

This recipe can be made as a vegetarian dish – just omit the mince and add extra vegetables instead.

1   Preheat the oven to 180°C (350°F). Lightly oil a large ovenproof dish.

2   Slice the zucchini in half crossways, then slice a small round off each half and set aside to use as lids to enclose the stuffing. Remove the insides of the zucchini using a knife and a spoon, leaving a 2 mm (⅛ inch) border (this can be tough, but stick at it!). Place the zucchini shells in the ovenproof dish and put the scooped-out flesh in the bowl of a food processor.

3   Slice off and reserve the eggplant tops. Remove the insides of the eggplants, leaving a 2 mm (⅛ inch) border. Add the shells to the dish with the zucchini. Add the eggplant flesh to the food processor bowl with the zucchini flesh and blitz until finely chopped.

4   Heat the olive oil in a large frying pan over medium heat and cook the onion, garlic, chilli, mint and parsley for 3–4 minutes or until the onion is translucent. Stir in the chopped zucchini and eggplant and season with salt and freshly ground black pepper. Cook for a further 3 minutes.

5   Add the beef mince and break it up into smaller pieces. Cook for about 10 minutes or until the mince has browned and cooked through and there is minimal liquid at the base of the pan. Season again with salt and pepper. Stir in the crushed tomatoes, tomato paste and oregano and cook until heated through. Add the rice and cook, stirring, for 2–3 minutes (it will finish cooking in the oven). Remove from the heat.

6   Fill the zucchini and eggplant shells with the beef mixture, add the vegetable lids and secure each one with a toothpick. Season the zucchini and eggplant with salt and pepper and drizzle with olive oil. Tightly cover the dish with foil and bake for 45–50 minutes or until the vegetables are tender.

Roasted seed pesto

Prep time: 10 minutes
Cook time: 10 minutes
Makes about 2 cups

¼ cup (40 g) pepitas
   (pumpkin seeds)
¼ cup (40 g) sunflower seeds
4 cups (200 g) baby spinach
1 cup firmly packed (50 g)
   basil leaves
½ cup (50 g) grated parmesan
   cheese
1–2 garlic cloves
Juice of ½ lemon
200 ml (7 fl oz) extra virgin
   olive oil

This is a great nut-free pesto. It's amazing spread on pizza bases or stirred through pasta. Make a jar for a friend who usually avoids pesto due to a nut allergy – they'll love it!

1   Preheat the grill to high (200°C/400°F). Spread the pepitas and sunflower seeds on a baking tray in a single layer. Cook for 1–2 minutes at a time, watching closely so they don't burn. Shuffle the seeds around and continue cooking until lightly browned. This may take up to 10 minutes. Set aside to cool.

2   Blitz the spinach, basil, parmesan, garlic, lemon juice, olive oil and the roasted seeds in a food processor until chopped to your liking – I like my pesto a little chunky, but keep blitzing if you prefer a smoother pesto.

3   Transfer the pesto to a jar and seal. Store it in the fridge for up to a week or freeze in an airtight container for up to 3 months.

EASY
&
DELI~~~~~

2

EASY &
DELICIOUS

-CIOUS

My two favourite things when it comes to recipes!

Spicy deconstructed lasagne

Prep time: 10 minutes
Cook time: 25 minutes
Serves 6

2 tablespoons olive oil
1 brown onion, finely diced
3 garlic cloves, crushed
1 small chilli, finely diced
500 g (1 lb 2 oz) spicy
    Italian sausages
700 ml (24 fl oz) tomato
    passata (puréed tomatoes)
1 tablespoon dried oregano
Pinch of salt
Pinch of freshly ground black
    pepper
2 teaspoons mustard powder
2 cups (500 ml) chicken stock
¼ cup (60 ml) thickened cream
300 g (10½ oz) dried lasagne
    sheets
Basil leaves, to serve

CHEESE TOPPING

½ cup (115 g) ricotta cheese
½ cup (65 g) grated mozzarella
    cheese
½ cup (50 g) grated parmesan
    cheese
⅓ cup basil leaves, finely
    chopped

This dish has all the flavour of a lasagne, without the need for layering and baking. For a leaner version, use beef mince instead of the Italian sausages. You may need to increase the seasonings as the sausages will be flavoured with Italian seasoning, which contributes to the overall flavour.

1   Heat the olive oil in a deep saucepan over medium heat. Cook the onion, garlic and chilli for 3–4 minutes or until the onion is translucent.

2   Remove the sausage meat from the casings and add it to the pan. Cook for 5–6 minutes, breaking the sausages into smaller pieces. Stir in the passata, oregano, salt, pepper, mustard powder and stock and cook until heated through. Pour in the cream and bring to a simmer.

3   Roughly snap the dried lasagne sheets straight into the pan and stir to ensure they don't stick together. Cook for 5–7 minutes or until the lasagne sheets are al dente.

4   Meanwhile, make the cheese topping. Add the cheeses and basil to a small bowl and mix well.

5   Spoon the lasagne mixture into serving bowls and add a spoonful of the cheese topping to each. Serve sprinkled with basil leaves.

Chicken katsu and soba noodle salad

Prep time: 20 minutes
Cook time: 20 minutes
Serves 2

---

2 skinless, boneless chicken
  breasts
⅓ cup (50 g) plain (all-purpose)
  flour
⅔ cup (50 g) panko breadcrumbs
1 egg
2 tablespoons tamari or
  soy sauce
1 tablespoon rice vinegar
3 teaspoons shiro miso paste
2 teaspoons sesame oil
2 teaspoons grated ginger
2 teaspoons honey
½ bunch garlic chives, finely
  chopped (see Tip)
180 g (6 oz) soba noodles
150 g (5½ oz) sugar snap peas
1 cup (155 g) frozen broad
  beans, thawed and peeled
Peanut oil, for frying

TONKATSU SAUCE
1 tablespoon tomato sauce
3 teaspoons apple sauce
3 teaspoons Worcestershire
  sauce
2 teaspoons oyster sauce

I went through a phase where I ate beef and soba noodle broth for lunch every day for two months! Here's another soba noodle dish I could become equally obsessed with. For a vegetarian meal, use firm tofu or a meat-free substitute instead of the chicken and omit the tonkatsu sauce.

1   Bring a saucepan of salted water to the boil.

2   Lightly pound the thick end of each chicken breast so that it is the same thickness as the other end. Season with salt and freshly ground black pepper.

3   Put the flour and breadcrumbs on separate plates. Whisk the egg in a bowl. Dredge the chicken pieces in the flour, then dip them in the egg and coat in the breadcrumbs. Set aside while you prepare the salad.

4   Combine the tamari, rice vinegar, miso, sesame oil, ginger, honey and garlic chives in a large bowl.

5   Cook the noodles in the boiling water for 2 minutes. Add the sugar snap peas and broad beans and cook for 1 minute, then drain. Rinse well under cold water and drain well.

6   Add the noodles, sugar snap peas and broad beans to the bowl with the tamari dressing and toss well to coat.

7   Pour enough of the peanut oil into a large frying pan to come 0.5–1 cm (¼–½ inch) up the side. Heat the oil over medium–high heat, then add the chicken and cook for 6–8 minutes on each side or until golden and cooked through. Remove from the pan, drain on paper towel and rest for a couple of minutes before slicing.

8   Meanwhile, make the tonkatsu sauce by combining all the ingredients in a small bowl.

9   Divide the salad among bowls, add the sliced chicken and spoon the tonkatsu sauce over the top.

Tip: If you can't find garlic chives, use regular chives and add 2 crushed garlic cloves.

Sumac pork and herbed labneh pita

Prep time: 10 minutes
Cook time: 15 minutes
Serves 2

1 tablespoon sumac
250 g (9 oz) pork fillet, trimmed
1 tablespoon olive oil
½ cup (130 g) labneh
⅓ cup chopped mixed herbs,
   such as mint, flat-leaf parsley
   and chives, plus extra to serve
1½ teaspoons honey
2 large wholemeal pita breads
½ small red capsicum (pepper),
   sliced
1 Lebanese (short) cucumber,
   sliced
1 tomato, sliced
¼ red onion, thinly sliced

Labneh (also known as labna) is a creamy yoghurt cheese. You could replace it with equal quantities of Greek-style yoghurt and cream cheese. For a gluten-free meal, use gluten-free pitas.

1   Sprinkle the sumac on a plate with some salt and freshly ground black pepper. Coat the pork fillet by rolling it in the mixture.

2   Heat the olive oil in a frying pan over medium heat and cook the pork for 12–15 minutes, turning to cook on all sides. Set aside to rest before slicing.

3   While the pork is cooking, combine the labneh, chopped herbs and honey in a small bowl and season with salt and freshly ground black pepper.

4   Spread the herbed labneh on the pita breads, top with the sliced pork and vegetables and sprinkle with the extra herbs. Roll up to serve.

Sfiha with roasted vegetables

Prep time: 20 minutes
Cook time: 40 minutes
Serves 2

---

1 zucchini (courgette), sliced
    on the diagonal
1 small red capsicum (pepper),
    chopped
300 g (10½ oz) kent pumpkin
    (squash), seeds removed,
    cut into wedges
Olive oil spray
1 cup (150 g) wholemeal
    self-raising flour, plus extra
    for dusting
½ cup (130 g) Greek-style
    yoghurt
250 g (9 oz) beef mince
½ brown onion, roughly
    chopped
1 garlic clove, crushed
1 handful flat-leaf parsley leaves
1½ tablespoons pomegranate
    molasses
1 tablespoon tomato paste
    (concentrated purée)
1½ teaspoons ground allspice
2 tablespoons pine nuts
3 teaspoons dukkah
Hummus, to serve

This is such a comforting meal when you're craving veggies. For a vegetarian version, you could use a meat substitute in place of the beef. For dairy-free sfiha, use coconut yoghurt.

1   Preheat the oven to 200°C (400°F). Line three baking trays with baking paper. Place the zucchini, capsicum and pumpkin on one of the trays. Spray with olive oil and season with salt and freshly ground black pepper. Roast for 20–25 minutes or until cooked.

2   Meanwhile, mix the flour, yoghurt and a generous pinch of salt together to make a dough. Form the dough into a ball and turn it out onto a lightly floured surface. Knead for a few minutes until smooth, then set aside.

3   Place the beef mince, onion, garlic, parsley, pomegranate molasses, tomato paste and allspice in a food processor and season with salt and pepper. Blitz to form a paste.

4   Divide the dough into two balls. Roll out on a lightly floured surface to form two 22 cm (8½ inch) circles. Transfer each dough circle to a separate baking tray, spread with the meat mixture and sprinkle with the pine nuts. Bake for 15 minutes or until the dough is cooked and the edges are golden.

5   Top each sfiha with the roasted vegetables, sprinkle with the dukkah and serve with hummus.

Cheat's falafel burgers with zhoug sauce

Prep time: 25 minutes
Cook time: 35 minutes
Serves 4

2 x 400 g (14 oz) tins
   chickpeas, rinsed and
   drained well
1 brown onion, chopped
4 garlic cloves, crushed
1 bunch flat-leaf parsley,
   leaves chopped
1½ teaspoons ground cumin
3 teaspoons ground coriander
¼ cup (30 g) chickpea flour
   (besan)
1 teaspoon baking powder
Olive oil spray
4 burger buns
⅔ cup (140 g) hummus
2 Lebanese (short) cucumbers,
   sliced
2 tomatoes, sliced
4 handfuls rocket (arugula)

ZHOUG SAUCE
¼ cup (60 ml) extra virgin
   olive oil
2 tablespoons lemon juice
1 bunch coriander (cilantro),
   leaves picked
1 jalapeño chilli, chopped
1 garlic clove, crushed
2 teaspoons ground cumin
1 teaspoon ground cardamom

Tinned chickpeas aren't generally used to make falafel because they often break up when frying. However, they do save time (soaking is boring!) and because these falafel are baked, they work well here.

1 Preheat the oven to 200°C (400°F). Line a baking tray with baking paper.

2 Place the chickpeas, onion, garlic, parsley, spices, chickpea flour and baking powder in a food processor and season with salt and freshly ground black pepper. Pulse to combine.

3 Generously spray the lined baking tray with olive oil. Shape the falafel mixture into four patties to fit the burger buns, place on the tray and spray the tops with olive oil. Bake for 20 minutes, then carefully turn the patties. Cook for 10–15 minutes or until crisp and golden.

4 Meanwhile, rinse and dry the food processor to make the zhoug sauce. Blitz the olive oil, lemon juice, coriander, chilli, garlic, cumin and cardamom to form a sauce. Season with salt and pepper.

5 To assemble, toast the split burger buns, then spread the insides with hummus. Top each base with a falafel patty, some cucumber and tomato, a generous amount of zhoug and the rocket. Finish with the bun tops and serve immediately.

Tip: Remove the jalapeño seeds for a milder sauce.

Sesame pork noodles

Prep time: 15 minutes, plus
  10 minutes soaking
Cook time: 25 minutes
Serves 4

---

250 g (9 oz) dangmyeon (glass)
  noodles (see Tips)
¼ cup (60 ml) gochujang
  (see Tips)
¼ cup (60 ml) soy sauce
2 tablespoons sesame seeds
1½ tablespoons sesame oil,
  plus extra for cooking eggs
1 tablespoon peanut oil
500 g (1 lb 2 oz) pork mince
150 g (5½ oz) shiitake
  mushrooms, sliced
1 white onion, sliced
2 garlic cloves, crushed
4 cups (200 g) baby spinach
4 eggs
Kimchi, to serve

Noodles are such a delicious, quick-and-easy dinner that's filling and super satisfying. I also love cooking noodles for guests as a starter to a bigger meal – they're always a hit!

1   Put the noodles in a heatproof bowl and cover generously with boiling water. Soak for 8–10 minutes or until soft. Drain and rinse under cold water.

2   Combine the gochujang, soy sauce and ¼ cup (60 ml) water in a small bowl. Set aside.

3   Toast the sesame seeds in a large dry frying pan over medium–high heat. Transfer to a bowl and return the pan to the heat.

4   Increase the heat to high. Add the sesame oil, peanut oil and pork to the pan. Brown the pork for 5 minutes, breaking it up with a spoon as it cooks. Add the mushrooms, onion and garlic and cook for 5 minutes. Stir in the sauce, then add the baby spinach and cook until wilted. Add the noodles and toss well to combine. Cover and keep warm while you cook the eggs.

5   Fry the eggs in a little more sesame oil over medium–high heat for a couple of minutes or until the whites are set but the yolks are still runny (or until cooked to your liking).

6   Serve the noodles topped with a fried egg, kimchi and toasted sesame seeds.

Tips: Dangmyeon are traditional Korean noodles made from sweet potato starch. They are also called glass or cellophane noodles. You can find them in large supermarkets or Asian grocery stores, but you can also substitute bean thread vermicelli or egg noodles.

Gochujang is a spicy Korean chilli paste. Look for it in large supermarkets or Asian grocery stores. If unavailable, you can use a mild sriracha sauce.

Chicken and cashew patties

Prep time: 30 minutes
Cook time: 15 minutes
Serves 4–6

Juice of ½ lemon
1 fennel bulb, shaved (see Tips)
400 g (14 oz) snow peas
   (mange tout)
2 teaspoons white sesame seeds
2 teaspoons black sesame seeds
2 egg whites
800 g (1 lb 12 oz) chicken mince
½ cup (80 g) roasted cashews,
   chopped
¼ cup chopped garlic chives
   (see Tips)
1 handful Thai basil leaves,
   chopped
1 tablespoon peanut oil
2 tablespoons sesame oil
2 tablespoons apple cider
   vinegar
1 tablespoon honey
Lime wedges, to serve

I love recipes that can be used in different ways. These patties can be eaten on their own, with salad, on a burger or in a lettuce cup. They're great for everyone and especially good to freeze.

1   Fill a large bowl with iced water and add the lemon juice and shaved fennel.

2   Place the snow peas in a heatproof bowl and cover with boiling water. Leave for 30 seconds, then drain and add to the bowl with the fennel.

3   Toast the white and black sesame seeds in a large frying pan over medium–high heat for a few minutes or until golden. Transfer to a small bowl and set aside.

4   Whisk the egg whites in a bowl until foamy. Add the chicken mince, cashews, garlic chives, Thai basil and some salt and freshly ground black pepper and mix to combine. Using wet hands, shape the mixture into eight patties.

5   Return the frying pan to medium heat and add the peanut oil. Cook the chicken patties, turning once, for about 10 minutes or until golden brown and cooked through. Remove from the pan and drain on paper towel.

6   While the patties are cooking, combine the sesame oil, vinegar and honey in a large bowl and season with salt and pepper. Drain the snow peas and fennel well, then toss them with the dressing to coat.

7   Serve the hot patties with the salad, sprinkled with the toasted sesame seeds and with the lime wedges on the side.

Tips: I use a mandolin to shave the fennel. Placing the fennel in iced acidulated water prevents it from discolouring and also makes it curl and crisp up.

If you can't find garlic chives, use regular chives and add 2 crushed garlic cloves.

Hot-smoked salmon and asparagus barley risotto

Prep time: 10 minutes
Cook time: 1 hour
Serves 4

4 cups (1 litre) vegetable stock
1½ tablespoons olive oil
1 brown onion, chopped
1 fennel bulb, chopped
2 garlic cloves, crushed
1¼ cups (250 g) pearl barley, rinsed
1 cup (250 ml) dry white wine
300 g (10½ oz) hot-smoked salmon
2 bunches (about 300 g) asparagus, chopped
1½ tablespoons lemon juice

Cooked barley has a similar texture to brown rice, which means it's a good substitute for arborio rice in a risotto. Hot-smoked salmon is easy to use because it's already cooked, so it saves time and extra dishes!

1 Bring the stock and 2 cups (500 ml) water to the boil in a saucepan over high heat. Reduce the heat to low and cover.

2 Heat the olive oil in a large saucepan over medium–high heat. Cook the onion and chopped fennel for 5 minutes, then add the garlic and cook for a few more minutes. Stir in the barley and cook for a couple of minutes. Pour in the wine and cook for 5 minutes or until absorbed.

3 Reduce the heat to medium–low and add the hot stock, one ladleful at a time, stirring regularly and waiting for the stock to be absorbed before adding another ladleful. Cook for about 35 minutes or until the barley is al dente.

4 Meanwhile, remove and discard the salmon skin and flake the flesh. Stir the salmon, chopped asparagus and lemon juice through the cooked risotto and season with salt and freshly ground black pepper. Remove from the heat, cover and set aside for a few minutes before serving.

Tip: You can sprinkle the risotto with the reserved fennel fronds or some chopped dill.

Lemon and lime tuna cakes with creamy wombok slaw

Prep time: 25 minutes
Cook time: 15 minutes
Serves 4

---

800 g (1 lb 12 oz) fresh tuna
3 spring onions (scallions),
   chopped
Finely grated zest of 1 small
   lemon
Finely grated zest of 1 lime
2 egg whites
1½ tablespoons rice flour
1 teaspoon lemon pepper
   spice blend
2 tablespoons peanut oil

CREAMY WOMBOK SLAW
¼ cup (60 g) whole egg
   mayonnaise
¼ cup (70 g) Greek-style
   yoghurt
Juice of 1 small lemon
Juice of 1 lime
1 tablespoon wasabi paste,
   or to taste
½ wombok (Chinese cabbage),
   shredded
1 carrot, peeled into ribbons
1 handful mint leaves, chopped
2 spring onions (scallions),
   chopped
Ground white pepper, to taste

Fish cakes are one of my favourite things to order when I'm eating out, so of course I had to make my own. These have a lovely zing from the lemon and lime, and the creaminess of the slaw balances out the flavours.

1   To make the wombok slaw, whisk the mayonnaise, yoghurt, lemon juice, lime juice and wasabi in a large bowl. Add the wombok, carrot, mint and spring onion, season with salt and white pepper and toss to combine.

2   Cut the tuna into 1.5 cm (⅝ inch) cubes and place them in a bowl. Stir in the spring onion, lemon zest, lime zest, egg whites, rice flour and lemon pepper and season with salt. Shape the mixture into eight patties.

3   Heat half of the oil in a large frying pan over medium–high heat. Carefully place four tuna cakes in the pan and cook for 2½ minutes, then turn and cook for another 2–3 minutes or until golden brown on the outside but still pink in the centre. Remove from the pan, add the remaining peanut oil and cook the rest of the tuna cakes. Set aside to rest for a few minutes.

4   Serve the tuna cakes with the wombok slaw.

Tip: Use a vegetable peeler to peel the carrot into ribbons (or you could simply grate it).

Meatball and lentil curry

Prep time: 25 minutes
Cook time: 45 minutes
Serves 4–6

1½ tablespoons olive oil
1 brown onion, chopped
4 garlic cloves, crushed
2 tablespoons ground coriander
1 tablespoon ground cumin
1½ teaspoons ground ginger
1 teaspoon ground turmeric
1 cinnamon stick
2 tomatoes, seeded and
    chopped
1½ cups (325 g) green lentils,
    rinsed
3½ cups (875 ml) vegetable
    stock
1 cup (250 ml) coconut milk
1 sprig curry leaves, bruised
500 g (1 lb 2 oz) beef mince
1 egg
¼ cup (30 g) dried breadcrumbs
¼ cup (60 ml) soda water
2 spring onions (scallions),
    finely chopped
2 teaspoons garam masala
4 cups (200 g) baby spinach
Coriander (cilantro) sprigs,
    to serve
Naan bread, to serve

I love this recipe because it's hearty, and has such a variety of ingredients that make for a delicious, nutritious meal. For a vegan dish, omit the meatballs and add some cubed firm tofu and extra spinach. Use gluten-free breadcrumbs for a gluten-free version.

1   Heat the olive oil in a large saucepan over medium–high heat. Cook the onion for 5 minutes, then add the garlic, spices and tomato and cook for a couple of minutes or until fragrant.

2   Stir in the green lentils, stock, coconut milk and curry leaves. Bring to the boil, then reduce the heat to medium–low and simmer for 20 minutes while you make the meatballs.

3   Combine the beef mince, egg, breadcrumbs, soda water, spring onion and garam masala with some salt and freshly ground black pepper in a large bowl. Roll the mixture into 24 balls.

4   Gently drop the meatballs into the simmering lentils, cover and cook for 15 minutes or until the lentils are soft and the meatballs are cooked through.

5   Discard the curry leaves and the cinnamon stick. Stir in the spinach and cook until just wilted. Season with salt and pepper. Serve the curry with coriander sprigs and naan bread.

Za'atar chicken with green goddess sauce

Prep time: 15 minutes
Cook time: 25 minutes
Serves 4

---

4 boneless, skinless chicken
   breasts
½ cup (60 g) za'atar spice blend
2 bunches (about 300 g)
   broccolini
2 bunches (about 1 kg) Dutch
   or baby heirloom carrots,
   trimmed
2 parsnips, peeled and
   quartered lengthways
Olive oil spray

GREEN GODDESS SAUCE
⅔ cup (190 g) Greek-style
   yoghurt
½ bunch coriander (cilantro),
   leaves picked
½ bunch mint, leaves picked
½ bunch dill
2 tablespoons chopped chives
2 tablespoons lemon juice
2 tablespoons baby capers,
   rinsed
1 small garlic clove, crushed

This green goddess sauce is seriously amazing! It's really good with chicken, but also with fish and red meat, so I suggest you make extra and save some. For a vegan version, use firm tofu in place of the chicken and coconut yoghurt instead of the Greek yoghurt.

1   Preheat the oven to 200°C (400°F). Line a baking tray with baking paper.

2   Press the chicken breasts into the za'atar to coat on both sides and place on the baking tray. Scatter the vegetables around the chicken, making sure the parsnips are on top of the other vegetables so they colour while cooking. Spray the chicken and vegetables with olive oil and season with salt and freshly ground black pepper. Roast for 20–25 minutes or until the chicken is cooked through. Set aside to rest for 5 minutes before slicing.

3   While the chicken is cooking, make the sauce by putting all of the ingredients in a blender and blending until smooth. Season with salt and pepper.

4   Serve the sliced chicken and roasted vegetables with the green goddess sauce spooned over the top.

Creamy pumpkin, spinach and walnut pappardelle

Prep time: 15 minutes
Cook time: 30 minutes
Serves 4

750 g (1 lb 10 oz) butternut
  pumpkin (squash)
1½ tablespoons (30 g) butter
1 brown onion, chopped
4 garlic cloves, peeled
2 tablespoons chopped sage
1 tablespoon thyme leaves
1⅔ cups (420 ml) vegetable
  stock
¾ cup (90 g) walnuts
500 g (1 lb 2 oz) pappardelle
  pasta
⅓ cup (85 g) crème fraîche
4 cups (200 g) baby spinach
Grated parmesan cheese,
  to serve

If you love pasta, you'll love this light and creamy dish that will satisfy the whole family. For a vegan meal, use a vegan cream and butter substitute. Use gluten-free pasta for a gluten-free version.

1 Preheat the oven to 180°C (350°F). Bring a large saucepan of salted water to the boil.

2 Peel the pumpkin and cut it into small pieces. Melt the butter in a saucepan over medium–high heat. Add the pumpkin, onion, garlic, sage and thyme and cook for 8–10 minutes or until beginning to colour. Pour in the stock and bring to the boil. Reduce the heat to medium–low, cover and cook for 15 minutes or until the pumpkin is soft.

3 Meanwhile, tumble the walnuts onto a baking tray and roast for 6–8 minutes or until golden and fragrant. Set aside to cool before chopping.

4 Add the pasta to the boiling water and cook according to the packet instructions. Drain well and return to the saucepan.

5 Remove the pumpkin mixture from the heat and stir in the crème fraîche. Use a stick blender to purée the sauce until velvety smooth, then season with salt and freshly ground black pepper.

6 Pour the pumpkin sauce over the pasta, add the spinach and toss well to coat the pasta and wilt the spinach. Serve topped with the chopped walnuts and grated parmesan.

Yakitori with quick pickled salad

Prep time: 30 minutes, plus
   30 minutes marinating
Cook time: 20 minutes
Serves 4

½ cup (125 ml) mirin
½ cup (125 ml) sake
½ cup (125 ml) tamari or.
   soy sauce
2 tablespoons honey
2 garlic cloves, crushed
2 teaspoons finely grated ginger
750 g (1 lb 10 oz) boneless,
   skinless chicken thighs

QUICK PICKLED SALAD
¾ cup (185 ml) rice vinegar
2 tablespoons honey
1 tablespoon salt
1 carrot, peeled
300 g (10½ oz) daikon, peeled
2 Lebanese (short) cucumbers
1 bunch (about 250 g) radishes
2 spring onions (scallions)

Pairing a deliciously marinated meat with a salty, sweet pickled salad is magical! If you're in a hurry, you can cook the thigh fillets whole instead of skewering them – this will save you loads of time.

1   Soak 12 wooden skewers in cold water to stop them from burning while cooking.

2   For the salad, whisk ¾ cup (185 ml) water with the vinegar, honey and salt until the honey has dissolved.

3   Use a vegetable peeler to peel the carrot and daikon into ribbons. Slice the cucumbers, radishes and spring onions. Add the vegetables and pickling liquid to a large resealable plastic bag. Expel the air, seal the bag and marinate in the fridge for 30 minutes.

4   Meanwhile, whisk the mirin, sake, tamari, honey, garlic and ginger in a small saucepan over medium–high heat. Bring to a simmer and cook for 5–8 minutes or until the sauce has reduced and thickened slightly. Set aside half of the sauce in a small bowl to use as a dipping sauce.

5   Heat a barbecue or chargrill pan over medium–high heat.

6   Cut the chicken thighs into 2.5 cm (1 inch) wide strips and thread them back and forth onto the soaked skewers. Grill the chicken for 1–2 minutes, then turn and baste the cooked side with the remaining sauce. Repeat the turning and basting until the chicken is almost cooked through, then turn and cook one final time without basting.

7   Serve the yakitori with the reserved dipping sauce and the drained pickled salad.

Tuna, preserved lemon and cannellini bean salad

Prep time: 15 minutes
Cook time: 5 minutes
Serves 2

1½ tablespoons olive oil
2 x 200 g (7 oz) tuna steaks
400 g (14 oz) tin cannellini
  beans, rinsed and drained
150 g (5½ oz) baby tomatoes,
  halved
1 bunch flat-leaf parsley,
  leaves picked

DRESSING
2 tablespoons extra virgin
  olive oil
2 tablespoons finely chopped
  preserved lemon rind
1 tablespoon white wine vinegar
1 teaspoon honey

'EVERYTHING BAGEL'
SEASONING
1½ tablespoons white sesame
  seeds
3 teaspoons black sesame seeds
1 teaspoon poppy seeds
1½ teaspoons dried garlic flakes
2 teaspoons dried onion flakes
2 teaspoons sea salt flakes

The tuna in this colourful salad has a secret weapon – it's coated with a classic 'everything bagel' seasoning. Make extra seasoning to store in an airtight container and use it on smashed avocado toast, chicken, fish, buddha bowls, and so on.

1 To make the seasoning, combine the sesame seeds, poppy seeds, garlic flakes, onion flakes and sea salt in a shallow bowl.

2 Heat the olive oil in a frying pan over medium–high heat. Press both sides of the tuna into the seasoning, then place in the pan and cook for 1 minute on each side for rare or until cooked to your liking. Set the tuna aside to rest before cutting it into bite-sized cubes.

3 Make the dressing by whisking the extra virgin olive oil, lemon rind, vinegar, honey and some salt and freshly ground black pepper in a large bowl.

4 Gently toss the cannellini beans, tomatoes, parsley and tuna in the dressing and serve immediately.

Lasagne primavera

Prep time: 30 minutes
Cook time: 50 minutes
Serves 6–8

2 bunches (about 300 g)
   asparagus, chopped
1 cup (130 g) frozen baby peas
150 g (5½ oz) sugar snap peas,
   chopped
500 g (1 lb 2 oz) frozen spinach,
   thawed and well drained
2 zucchini (courgettes), grated
1 bunch chives, chopped
4 cups (920 g) ricotta cheese
1½ cups (150 g) finely grated
   parmesan cheese
1⅓ cups (330 ml) vegetable
   stock
2 teaspoons finely grated
   lemon zest
6 fresh lasagne sheets
1½ cups (190 g) grated
   mozzarella cheese

PESTO

⅓ cup (50 g) pine nuts
2 bunches basil, leaves picked
1 cup (100 g) finely grated
   parmesan cheese
½ cup (125 ml) extra virgin
   olive oil
4 garlic cloves, crushed

Who doesn't love lasagne? Adding more veggies as I've done here and switching up the flavours is a great way to get creative in the kitchen. Use store-bought basil pesto for a shortcut – you will need 1¼ cups (310 g). You can use gluten-free lasagne sheets for a gluten-free meal.

1   Preheat the oven to 180°C (350°F).

2   For the pesto, spread the pine nuts on a baking tray and roast for 5 minutes or until golden. Tip the pine nuts into a food processor and add the basil, parmesan, olive oil and garlic. Blitz until the mixture reaches the consistency of pesto. Season with salt and freshly ground black pepper.

3   Combine the asparagus, peas, sugar snap peas, spinach, zucchini and chives in a large bowl and season with salt and pepper.

4   Using electric beaters, beat the ricotta, parmesan, stock and lemon zest until combined. Season with salt and pepper.

5   Spoon a quarter of the ricotta mixture over the base of a 20 x 30 cm (8 x 12 inch) ovenproof dish. Top with 2 lasagne sheets. Spread a third of the pesto over the pasta, then add half of the vegetable mixture and top with another quarter of the ricotta mixture and 2 lasagne sheets. Repeat the layers, finishing with the lasagne sheets. Dollop the remaining ricotta mixture and pesto over the top. Sprinkle the mozzarella over the lasagne.

6   Bake the lasagne for 40–45 minutes or until bubbling and golden. Remove from the oven and set aside to rest in the dish for 10 minutes before serving.

Crispy mustard chicken with gruyere roasted broccoli

Prep time: 20 minutes
Cook time: 40 minutes
Serves 4

¼ cup (60 ml) olive oil
6 garlic cloves, crushed
2 tablespoons thyme leaves
⅓ cup (90 g) dijon mustard
8 small chicken thighs, bone in
  and skin on
1 cup (60 g) panko breadcrumbs
750 g (1 lb 10 oz) broccoli
1 cup (80 g) finely grated
  gruyere cheese

Anything crispy is a 'yes' in my book, and this chicken is the perfect dinner. Mustard and cheese is such a good combo that this meal will be a winner with the whole family.

1 Preheat the oven to 200°C (400°F). Line a large baking tray with baking paper.

2 Combine the olive oil, garlic and thyme in a large bowl with some salt and freshly ground black pepper. Add 2 tablespoons of the mixture to a medium bowl and set aside.

3 Stir the mustard into the remaining garlic mixture in the large bowl. Add the chicken thighs and toss well to coat.

4 Pour the breadcrumbs onto a plate. Press each chicken thigh into the crumbs, skin side down, then place on the baking tray, crumb side up. Roast in the oven for 20 minutes.

5 Meanwhile, cut the broccoli in half along the stalk and up through the head. Cut it into long, evenly sized florets with the stalk attached. Add the broccoli to the medium bowl with the garlic and thyme oil and toss well to coat.

6 Remove the chicken from the oven, add the broccoli to the tray and sprinkle the grated cheese over the broccoli. Roast the chicken and broccoli for a further 15–20 minutes or until the chicken is golden and cooked through and the broccoli is tender.

Sweet potato gnocchi with speck and rainbow chard

Prep time: 15 minutes
Cook time: 20 minutes
Serves 4

8 rainbow chard stalks
¼ cup (60 g) butter
2½ tablespoons olive oil
1 large bunch sage, leaves picked
180 g (6 oz) speck, diced
4 garlic cloves, crushed
500 g (1 lb 2 oz) sweet potato
  gnocchi
Shaved parmesan cheese,
  to serve

Using sweet potato gnocchi is a great way to add a little extra flavour to a pasta meal – plus it adds some colour! If you can't find rainbow chard, use silverbeet (Swiss chard). You can also use streaky bacon instead of speck.

1   Bring a large saucepan of salted water to the boil.

2   Roughly chop the chard leaves and slice the stems into 1 cm (½ inch) pieces.

3   Heat the butter and oil in a large frying pan over medium–high heat. Cook the sage leaves for a few minutes until they have darkened in colour. Remove with a slotted spoon and drain on paper towel.

4   Cook the speck in the same pan for 5 minutes or until crisp. Add the garlic along with the chard stems and leaves and cook for 8–10 minutes or until wilted. Season with salt and freshly ground black pepper.

5   Meanwhile, add the gnocchi to the boiling water and cook according to the packet instructions. Drain well, add to the pan with the speck and chard and cook for a couple of minutes to bring all the flavours together.

6   Serve the gnocchi topped with shaved parmesan and the crispy sage leaves.

Harissa prawn noodles

Prep time: 25 minutes
Cook time: 15 minutes
Serves 4

---

200 g (7 oz) rice vermicelli
   or bean thread noodles
¾ cup (185 ml) coconut milk
¼ cup (60 ml) vegetable stock
¼ cup (60 ml) tamari or
   soy sauce
1 tablespoon brown sugar
2 tablespoons finely grated
   ginger
1½ tablespoons harissa paste
6 garlic cloves, crushed
24 raw prawns, peeled and
   deveined, tails on
2 tablespoons peanut oil
1 bunch (about 240 g) Chinese
   broccoli, cut into bite-sized
   pieces
1 bunch (about 150 g) broccolini,
   cut into bite-sized pieces
1 carrot, peeled and julienned
4 spring onions (scallions),
   chopped
150 g (5½ oz) snow peas
   (mange tout), halved
1 bunch Thai basil, leaves picked
1 bunch coriander (cilantro),
   leaves chopped
2 tablespoons lime juice, plus
   lime wedges to serve

These have such a lovely flavour and they smell incredible while they're cooking. For something a little different, you can marinate the prawns, thread them onto skewers and cook them on the barbecue. For a vegan version, substitute firm tofu for the prawns.

1   Prepare the noodles according to the packet instructions.

2   Add the coconut milk, stock, tamari and sugar to a small bowl and mix to combine. Set aside.

3   Combine the ginger, harissa and garlic in a bowl. Pat the prawns dry with paper towel, add them to the bowl and stir well to coat.

4   Heat the peanut oil in a large frying pan or wok over high heat. Cook the prawns for a few minutes or until almost cooked through. Remove the prawns from the pan and set aside.

5   Add ¼ cup (60 ml) water to the harissa mixture remaining in the pan and stir to loosen any residue. Add the Chinese broccoli, broccolini, carrot and half of the chopped spring onion. Cook for a few minutes before adding the coconut milk mixture. Boil the sauce for 1 minute, then return the prawns to the pan and add the noodles, snow peas, remaining spring onion, Thai basil, coriander and lime juice. Gently toss to combine.

6   Season with salt and serve with lime wedges.

Zoodle pasta carbonara

Prep time: 15 minutes
Cook time: 20 minutes
Serves 2

---

1 small zucchini (courgette)
2 teaspoons olive oil
100 g (3½ oz) pancetta,
    chopped
1 garlic clove, crushed
200 g (7 oz) spaghetti or
    pasta of your choice
Olive oil spray
1 egg
1 egg yolk
½ cup (50 g) finely grated
    parmesan cheese, plus
    extra to serve
Chopped flat-leaf parsley,
    to serve

Zucchini noodles are a great way to get more veggies into your diet. If you're like me and love pasta, using half pasta and half zoodles is a simple way to enjoy those delicious carbohydrates while also adding the extra veg. You could replace the zoodles with spaghetti squash when it's in season.

1   Make the zoodles by spiralising the zucchini using a spiraliser, or use a vegetable peeler to cut it into fettuccine-style strips. Place the zoodles in a colander, sprinkle with salt and set aside for 10 minutes to draw out the excess liquid. Pat the zoodles dry with paper towel.

2   Bring a large saucepan of water to the boil.

3   Meanwhile, heat the oil in a large frying pan over medium–high heat and cook the pancetta for 5 minutes. Add the garlic and cook for 1 minute. Remove the pan from the heat.

4   Add the pasta to the boiling water and cook according to the packet instructions. Drain well and return to the pan, reserving ¼ cup (60 ml) of the water.

5   Spray the frying pan with olive oil (unless there is still some oil remaining in the pan) and return the pan to medium heat. Add the zoodles and cook for 2–4 minutes or until tender, then add the drained pasta and mix well.

6   Whisk the egg, egg yolk, parmesan and 1½ tablespoons water in a small bowl. Season with freshly ground black pepper.

7   Pour the egg mixture into the pan with the zoodles and pasta and cook, stirring, for 3–5 minutes. Add the pasta water and continue stirring until thickened and creamy (do not rush this step or the eggs will scramble). Season with salt and pepper and serve topped with the parsley and extra parmesan.

Char siu pork wraps

Prep time: 10 minutes
Cook time: 10 minutes
Serves 2

---

1 tablespoon peanut oil
250 g (9 oz) pork mince
1 small red capsicum (pepper),
    sliced
2 teaspoons finely grated ginger
2 garlic cloves, crushed
¼ cup (60 ml) char siu sauce
1 tablespoon soy sauce
⅓ cup (50 g) water chestnuts,
    chopped
1 handful coriander (cilantro),
    chopped
6 white corn tortillas
1 Lebanese (short) cucumber,
    halved lengthways and sliced
2 spring onions (scallions),
    julienned

Ten-minute meals are my favourite, and these wraps are such a goody for lunch or dinner. If you want a lighter version, you can use lettuce cups instead of tortillas.

1   Heat the peanut oil in a frying pan over medium–high heat. Cook the pork, capsicum, ginger and garlic for 5 minutes, breaking up the pork with a spoon as it cooks.

2   Stir in the char siu sauce, soy sauce and water chestnuts. Simmer for a couple of minutes, then remove the pan from the heat and stir in the coriander.

3   Warm the tortillas according to the packet instructions.

4   Spoon the char siu pork onto the tortillas, top with the cucumber slices and spring onion, roll up and serve.

Chu hou chilli chicken salad

Prep time: 15 minutes
Cook time: 15 minutes
Serves 2

---

2 skinless, boneless chicken
     breasts
⅓ cup (80 ml) chu hou sauce
1 teaspoon chilli powder
     (see Tips)
1 tablespoon peanut oil
1½ tablespoons rice vinegar
1½ tablespoons soy sauce
2 teaspoons honey
2 teaspoons sesame oil
¼ wombok (Chinese cabbage),
     shredded
1 carrot, peeled and julienned
1 avocado, chopped
3 spring onions (scallions),
     chopped
½ cup (100 g) crispy fried
     noodles (see Tips)

I love chicken salads, and with all these veggies and amazing flavours, this is my favourite! Chu hou sauce is a fermented bean paste. If you can't find it, you can use hoisin sauce, which is more readily available in supermarkets. For a vegan meal, use firm tofu instead of chicken and sugar instead of honey.

1 Cut the chicken into 1 cm (½ inch) thick strips.

2 Combine the chu hou sauce, chilli powder and peanut oil in a bowl. Add the chicken strips and toss well to coat. Set aside to marinate for 10 minutes.

3 Meanwhile, combine the rice vinegar, soy sauce, honey and sesame oil in a large bowl. Add the wombok, carrot, avocado, spring onion and crispy noodles and gently toss to combine.

4 Place a large non-stick frying pan over medium–high heat. Cook the chicken strips for 2–3 minutes on each side or until cooked through.

5 Spoon the salad onto serving plates and top with the chicken.

Tips: Chilli powders vary greatly in intensity, so add more or less depending on your taste.

Crispy fried noodles are ready-to-eat noodles that are great for adding crunch to Asian-style salads. Look for them in the noodle section of the supermarket.

Korean-inspired beef with zucchini noodle salad

Prep time: 15 minutes, plus
   30 minutes marinating
Cook time: 10 minutes
Serves 2

½ small red onion, very thinly
   sliced
⅓ cup (80 ml) apple cider
   vinegar
¼ cup (60 ml) tamari or
   soy sauce
2 tablespoons brown sugar
1 teaspoon ground ginger
1 garlic clove, crushed
1 tablespoon sesame oil
2 x 200 g (7 oz) beef eye
   fillet steaks
1½ tablespoons sriracha hot
   chilli sauce
1½ tablespoons maple syrup
3 zucchini (courgettes)
1 tablespoon peanut oil
½ bunch coriander (cilantro),
   chopped
⅓ cup (50 g) cashews, roughly
   chopped

When I'm feeling like something light but super flavoursome, this is my go-to dinner! Swap out the beef fillet for chicken breast for a budget-friendly alternative.

1 Place the onion and vinegar in a small bowl with a couple of generous pinches of salt. Set aside for at least 30 minutes.

2 Meanwhile, combine the tamari, brown sugar, ginger, garlic and half of the sesame oil in a bowl. Add the beef and turn to coat. Set aside to marinate for at least 30 minutes, turning occasionally. (If you're leaving it for longer than 30 minutes, pop it in the fridge.)

3 Combine the sriracha, maple syrup and remaining sesame oil in a large bowl. Add 2 tablespoons of the soaking vinegar from the onion and season with salt and freshly ground black pepper.

4 Spiralise the zucchini or peel them into ribbons.

5 Heat the peanut oil in a frying pan over medium–high heat. Remove the beef from the marinade, reserving the marinade, and pat dry with paper towel. Cook for 2½–3 minutes on each side for medium or until cooked to your liking. Remove from the pan and set aside to rest.

6 Wipe out the pan with paper towel and return to the heat. Add the reserved marinade, bring to the boil and cook for 1–2 minutes or until thickened. Remove from the heat.

7 Slice the beef and drain the onion. Add the zucchini to the bowl with the sriracha dressing. Add most of the coriander and cashews and toss well to coat.

8 Divide the salad between serving plates and top it with the sliced beef, onion and remaining coriander and cashews. Serve drizzled with a little of the reduced marinade.

Tip: If you like your steak more well done than medium, reduce the temperature of the pan slightly so the marinade doesn't burn while the steaks cook through.

Pulled pork rolls with apple and daikon slaw

Prep time: 20 minutes
Cook time: 2¼ hours
Serves 8

1.2 kg (2 lb 11 oz) pork neck
2 teaspoons peanut oil
3 cups (750 ml) chicken stock
1 brown onion, quartered
1 celery stalk, quartered
4 garlic cloves, bruised
1 cm (½ inch) knob of ginger,
  sliced
2 bird's eye chillies, halved
2 lemongrass stalks, peeled
  and bruised
¼ cup (60 g) tamarind purée
2 tablespoons honey
2 tablespoons fish sauce
6 kaffir lime leaves, bruised
8 brioche buns, halved and
  lightly toasted

APPLE AND DAIKON SLAW

¼ cup (70 g) Greek-style
  yoghurt
¼ cup (60 g) whole egg
  mayonnaise
1½ tablespoons lime juice
1 bunch chives, chopped
2 green apples
200 g (7 oz) daikon, peeled
⅛ red cabbage, shredded
½ bunch mint, leaves roughly
  chopped
½ bunch coriander (cilantro),
  leaves roughly chopped

Pulled pork is always a crowd favourite. Using it to make pork rolls is a great way to mix things up, and the sweetness of the buns, pork and slaw means you don't need any extra sauce. A mandolin makes slicing the slaw ingredients quick and easy.

1 Preheat the oven to 160°C (315°F).

2 Cut the pork into three thick steaks and season with salt and freshly ground black pepper.

3 Heat the peanut oil in a large ovenproof saucepan over medium–high heat. Add the pork steaks and brown well on both sides. Add the stock, onion, celery, garlic, ginger, chilli, lemongrass, tamarind purée, honey, fish sauce and lime leaves. Bring to a simmer, cover and braise in the oven for 2 hours or until the pork is meltingly tender and easily pulls apart.

4 Meanwhile, make the apple and daikon slaw. Combine the yoghurt, mayonnaise, lime juice and chives with some salt and pepper in a large bowl. Cut the apple and daikon into julienne strips. Add the apple to the dressing and toss to coat. Add the daikon, cabbage, mint and coriander. Toss well to combine, then season with salt and pepper.

5 Shred the pork and place it in a bowl. Put the pan with the braising liquid over high heat and cook for 5 minutes or until the liquid has reduced and thickened slightly. Strain the liquid over the pork and stir to combine. Season with salt and pepper.

6 Top the brioche bases with the slaw and shredded pork, add the brioche lids and serve.

Tips: Coating the apples in the dressing first will help to prevent them from oxidising.

Hit the lemongrass all over with the back of a knife to bruise it.

Braised paprika chicken and lentils

Prep time: 10 minutes
Cook time: 50 minutes
Serves 4

---

1 tablespoon olive oil
8 small chicken thighs, bone
    in and skin on
1 brown onion, chopped
4 garlic cloves, crushed
1 tablespoon sweet paprika
150 g (5½ oz) marinated red
    capsicum (pepper), sliced
    (page 184)
400 g (14 oz) baby tomatoes
140 g (5 oz) chopped kale
¾ cup (185 ml) medium dry
    sherry
2 cups (500 ml) chicken stock
1 cup (210 g) French-style
    lentils
1 cup (125 g) pitted green olives
Chopped flat-leaf parsley,
    to serve

The lentils in this hearty and comforting family-style meal are a brilliant way to include extra protein and fibre, as well as some variety.

1 Preheat the oven to 180°C (350°F).

2 Heat the olive oil in a large ovenproof frying pan over high heat. Season the chicken with salt and freshly ground black pepper. Cook, skin side down, for 5 minutes or until golden. Remove from the pan and set aside.

3 Reduce the heat to medium and cook the onion for a few minutes, then add the garlic, paprika, capsicum, tomatoes and kale and cook for a few more minutes. Add the sherry and let it bubble away for a couple of minutes before adding the stock, lentils and olives. Bring to a simmer and cook for 10 minutes.

4 Place the chicken on top of the lentils and vegetables, skin side up and making sure the skin isn't covered. Braise in the oven for 25–30 minutes or until the chicken and lentils are cooked.

5 Serve sprinkled with chopped parsley.

Tips: If you're using large chicken thighs, you'll only need four, but you'll need to braise them for longer.

For a deeper olive flavour, use pitted kalamata olives.

Broccolini and smoked almond salad with lemon whiting

Prep time: 15 minutes
Cook time: 5 minutes
Serves 2

2 bunches (about 300 g)
   broccolini
2 teaspoons honey
Juice of 1 lemon
2 tablespoons Greek-style
   yoghurt
2 tablespoons whole egg
   mayonnaise
2 teaspoons dijon mustard
1 bunch chives, chopped
¼ cup (30 g) hemp seeds
¼ cup (40 g) smoked almonds,
   roughly chopped
4 whiting fillets or other small,
   firm white fish fillets
2 teaspoons olive oil

The smoked almonds add a special touch to this dish. They make every bite seriously delicious and they're so much tastier than regular almonds. For a dairy-free meal, use only mayonnaise in the dressing; for an egg-free meal, use only yoghurt. You can replace the whiting with haloumi for a vegetarian version.

1   Put the broccolini in a large bowl, cover with boiling water and set aside for 1½ minutes, then drain well and cool.

2   Add the honey and 2 tablespoons of the lemon juice to a large bowl and stir until the honey has dissolved. Add the yoghurt, mayonnaise, mustard and chives and season with salt and freshly ground black pepper.

3   Chop the broccolini into small pieces and add it to the bowl with the dressing. Add the hemp seeds and almonds and toss well to combine.

4   Season the fish with salt and pepper. Heat the olive oil in a frying pan over high heat and cook the fish, skin side down, for 3 minutes. Pour the remaining lemon juice over the fish, then turn and cook for another 30–60 seconds or until just cooked through.

5   Serve the fish with the broccolini and almond salad.

ITSINES

ITSINES
FAMILY
FAVOURITES

Favour-

FAMILY

ites

Our family dinners are a bit special ... and you're invited!

Yiayia's pastitsio

Prep time: 20 minutes
Cook time: 2 hours
Serves 6

---

2 tablespoons olive oil,
    plus extra for cooking
500 g (1 lb 2 oz) lean beef
    mince
¼ cup (60 ml) red wine
1 onion, finely diced
3 garlic cloves, crushed
1 tablespoon dried oregano
1 tablespoon rosemary,
    finely chopped
2 cloves
1 teaspoon ground allspice
1 tablespoon tomato paste
    (concentrated purée)
1 bay leaf
1 cinnamon stick
400 g (14 oz) tin crushed
    tomatoes
½ cup (125 ml) beef stock,
    as needed
250 g (9 oz) penne pasta
¾ cup (80 g) grated parmesan
    cheese

BÉCHAMEL SAUCE
¾ cup (185 g) butter
¾ cup (110 g) plain
    (all-purpose) flour
3 cups (750 ml) warm milk
2 eggs, lightly beaten
¾ cup (80 g) grated parmesan
    cheese
¼ teaspoon freshly grated
    nutmeg

This is one of our family favourites, which Yiayia makes on special occasions. For a vegetarian dish, omit the beef mince and add some extra vegetables, such as zucchini (courgette) or eggplant (aubergine).

1   Heat a splash of olive oil in a large non-stick frying pan over medium–high heat. Add the beef and cook until browned and the excess liquid has evaporated. Add the wine, onion, garlic, oregano, rosemary, cloves and allspice and cook for 5 minutes. Add the tomato paste, bay leaf, cinnamon stick and crushed tomatoes. Reduce the heat and simmer for 1 hour, adding the stock if the mixture is drying out. Season with salt and freshly ground black pepper.

2   While the meat is cooking, bring a large saucepan of salted water to the boil. Add the pasta and cook until al dente. Drain, then transfer to a bowl and toss with 2 tablespoons of the olive oil. Set aside to cool.

3   Preheat the oven to 200°C (400°F). Brush a large ovenproof dish with oil.

4   To make the béchamel sauce, melt the butter in a saucepan over medium heat. Add the flour and stir for 2 minutes, then remove the pan from the heat. Slowly add the milk, stirring until the mixture is smooth and thick. Cover and set aside to cool for 10 minutes. Stir in the eggs, parmesan and nutmeg.

5   Tip the pasta into the oiled dish and sprinkle with the parmesan. Pour the meat sauce over the top, followed by the béchamel. Bake for 45 minutes or until golden brown.

Greek lamb wraps with tzatziki salad

Prep time: 15 minutes
Cook time: 10 minutes
Serves 2

---

2 teaspoons dried oregano
1 teaspoon smoked paprika
½ teaspoon dried thyme
½ teaspoon ground cumin
2 garlic cloves, crushed
1 tablespoon olive oil
300 g (10½ oz) lamb backstrap
2 Greek pita breads

TZATZIKI SALAD

¼ cup (70 g) Greek-style
   yoghurt
1 tablespoon lemon juice
1 garlic clove, crushed
1 Lebanese (short) cucumber,
   halved lengthways and sliced
1 handful mint leaves, roughly
   chopped

For a dairy-free meal, substitute coconut yoghurt for the Greek-style yoghurt. For a gluten-free meal, use gluten-free pita breads.

1   Stir the oregano, paprika, thyme, cumin and garlic into the olive oil in a large shallow bowl. Season with salt and freshly ground black pepper. Roll the lamb around in the marinade to coat, then set aside while you make the salad.

2   For the salad, combine the yoghurt, lemon juice and garlic in a bowl. Stir in the cucumber and mint and season with salt and pepper.

3   Heat a frying pan over medium–high heat and cook the lamb for 3–4 minutes on each side or until done to your liking. Set aside to rest before slicing.

4   Meanwhile, warm the pitas in a dry frying pan or chargrill pan. Divide the tzatziki salad between the pitas and top with the sliced lamb. Roll up to serve.

Greek fasolakia with chicken

Prep time: 15 minutes
Cook time: 30 minutes
Serves 4

---

4 boneless, skinless chicken
   thighs
Olive oil, for cooking
1 brown onion, finely diced
2 garlic cloves, crushed
1 small red chilli, thinly sliced
4 large potatoes, peeled and
   quartered
500 g (1 lb 2 oz) string beans,
   topped and tailed
¼ cup flat-leaf parsley, finely
   chopped, plus extra parsley
   leaves to serve
2 cups (500 ml) chicken stock
400 g (14 oz) tin crushed
   tomatoes
2 tablespoons tomato paste
   (concentrated purée)
Crumbled feta cheese, to serve

This can be served with some basmati rice or toasted bread.
My yiayia always serves this with a fresh lettuce and spring
onion (scallion) salad.

1   Remove the excess fat from the chicken thighs.

2   Heat a splash of olive oil in a large deep saucepan over
    medium heat and cook the onion, garlic and chilli for
    3–4 minutes or until softened.

3   Add the chicken thighs and season with salt and freshly
    ground black pepper. Lightly brown for 2–3 minutes.
    Add the potato, beans and parsley and season again, then
    cook for another 2–3 minutes or until the vegetables
    begin to soften.

4   Stir in the stock, crushed tomatoes and tomato paste.
    Cover and simmer for 20 minutes or until the chicken
    is cooked through.

5   Serve the chicken and vegetables topped with crumbled
    feta cheese and extra parsley.

Chilli crab and prawn pasta

Prep time: 15 minutes
Cook time: 20 minutes
Serves 4

¼ cup (60 ml) olive oil
1 brown onion, finely diced
3 garlic cloves, crushed
1 small hot red chilli, finely
  chopped
¼ cup roughly chopped flat-leaf
  parsley
400 g (14 oz) cherry tomatoes
Grated zest and juice of 1 lemon
500 g (1 lb 2 oz) linguine pasta
16 raw banana prawns, peeled
  and deveined, tails on
150 g (5½ oz) blue swimmer
  crab meat
⅓ cup (35 g) grated parmesan
  cheese

I absolutely love this recipe – it's a firm family favourite. I love it with some extra heat, but you can adjust the chilli to taste. Substitute some baby squid or firm fish if you can't find the crab meat.

1   Heat the olive oil in a saucepan over medium heat. Add the onion, garlic, chilli and parsley, reduce the heat to low and cook for 5 minutes or until the onion is soft and translucent. Season with salt and freshly ground black pepper.

2   Stir in the tomatoes, lemon zest and lemon juice and return the heat to medium. Cook for 5–7 minutes or until the tomatoes begin to burst.

3   Meanwhile, bring a large saucepan of salted water to the boil. Add the pasta and cook according to the packet instructions.

4   Add the prawns and crab meat to the tomato mixture and cook for 5 minutes or until the prawns are cooked through. Add 1 cup (250 ml) of the pasta water to make a broth and stir in 2–3 tablespoons of the grated parmesan. The prawns should be almost submerged (depending on the pan you're using). Season well with salt and pepper.

5   Once the pasta is cooked, add it straight from the pan to the tomato mixture and stir to combine. Taste and season with salt and pepper.

6   Serve the pasta topped with the remaining parmesan.

Yiayia's bamyes

Prep time: 15 minutes,
    plus 45 minutes soaking
Cook time: 35 minutes
Serves 4

---

1 kg (2 lb 4 oz) okra
¾ cup (185 ml) white vinegar
Olive oil, for cooking
1 brown onion, finely diced
2 garlic cloves, crushed
1 small red chilli, thinly sliced
4 chicken thighs, bone in and
    skin on, excess fat removed
2 tablespoons tomato paste
    (concentrated purée)
400 g (14 oz) tin crushed
    tomatoes
1 cup (250 ml) chicken stock
Crumbled feta cheese, to serve
Toasted sourdough, to serve

I love this with some toasted crusty bread to mop up the juices. If you can't find okra, you can replace it with some green beans, zucchini (courgette) or eggplant (aubergine).

1   When cooking okra, you need to start by soaking it in a vinegar and water solution. Place the okra in a bowl and add the white vinegar. Fill the bowl with water and leave the okra to soak for about 45 minutes.

2   Drain the okra, rinse well and pat dry with paper towel. Cut off the stems.

3   Heat a splash of olive oil in a deep saucepan over medium heat. Add the onion, garlic and chilli and cook for 3–4 minutes or until softened. Add the chicken thighs and season with salt and freshly ground black pepper. Cook until browned all over.

4   Stir in the okra and tomato paste and cook for 1–2 minutes or until the okra is lightly golden. Add the crushed tomatoes and stock. Cover and simmer for 25 minutes or until the okra is tender and the chicken is completely cooked through.

5   Serve the chicken and vegetables topped with crumbled feta, with the toasted sourdough on the side.

One-pot chicken and rice

Prep time: 15 minutes
Cook time: 50 minutes
Serves 4–6

⅓ cup (80 ml) peanut oil
2 leeks, pale parts only, sliced
2 garlic cloves, crushed
½ cup (125 ml) Chinese cooking
  wine
4 cups (1 litre) chicken stock
2 cups (400 g) long-grain
  brown rice
2 star anise
1 kg (2 lb 4 oz) skinless,
  boneless chicken thighs
2 tablespoons grated ginger
3 spring onions (scallions),
  chopped
4 cups (200 g) baby spinach
⅔ cup (105 g) roasted cashews,
  roughly chopped
1 bunch coriander (cilantro),
  chopped

I love this easy one-pot dish – all of the beautiful flavours develop as it quietly simmers away, plus there's not much washing up at the end! It would make a perfect addition to your meal prep repertoire.

1   Heat 1 tablespoon of the peanut oil in a large saucepan over medium–high heat. Cook the leek with a generous pinch of salt for 6–8 minutes or until softened. Add the garlic and cook for 1 minute, then pour in the cooking wine and let it bubble away for 1 minute. Add the stock, rice and star anise, bring to the boil and cook for 15 minutes.

2   Add the chicken and return to the boil, then reduce the heat to low, cover and gently simmer for 20–25 minutes or until the rice and chicken are cooked.

3   Meanwhile, combine the ginger, spring onion and remaining peanut oil in a small bowl and generously season with salt.

4   Stir the spinach through the rice. Ladle the chicken and rice mixture into bowls, top with the cashews and coriander and serve with the ginger and spring onion sauce.

Tip: For ease of eating, you can remove the cooked chicken from the rice and slice it before serving.

Mum's salmon

Prep time: 10 minutes
Cook time: 15 minutes
Serves 4

4 skinless salmon fillets
Sweet paprika, for sprinkling
Olive oil, for cooking
2 small red chillies, roughly
  chopped
2 tablespoons coriander
  (cilantro) roots and stems
3 garlic cloves
1 lemongrass stalk, white
  part only
½ cup (125 ml) fish stock
¼ cup (60 ml) fish sauce
2 tablespoons soy sauce
Juice of 1 large lime
1 teaspoon brown sugar
2 cm (¾ inch) knob of ginger,
  cut into thin strips
Steamed rice or Chicken rice
  (page 181), to serve
Coriander (cilantro) leaves,
  for garnish
1 mild, long red chilli, finely
  chopped

Whenever Mum is cooking her salmon, we all rush to her house for dinner! It's light, but so delicious. This recipe also works well with white fish or firm tofu. It's lovely served with Chicken rice (page 181).

1   Preheat the oven to 200°C (400°F).

2   Season the salmon fillets with salt, freshly ground black pepper and a sprinkle of sweet paprika. Heat a splash of olive oil in a small non-stick frying pan over medium heat. Lightly brown the salmon fillets on each side, then place them in a deep ovenproof dish.

3   Combine the chilli, coriander, garlic and lemongrass in a small blender and blend until finely chopped. Add the fish stock, fish sauce, soy sauce, lime juice and brown sugar and blend until well combined.

4   Pour the sauce over the salmon, top with the ginger slices and bake for 10 minutes or until cooked to your liking.

5   Serve the salmon on a bed of rice, topped with the coriander and chilli.

Stuffed portobello mushrooms

Prep time: 20 minutes
Cook time: 30 minutes
Serves 4

---

150 g (5½ oz) wholemeal
   sourdough
½ cup (75 g) hazelnuts
1 cup (100 g) finely grated
   parmesan cheese
2 tablespoons olive oil
250 g (9 oz) frozen spinach,
   thawed and drained
1½ cups (450 g) ricotta cheese
2 teaspoons lemon juice
2 teaspoons thyme leaves
⅓ cup finely chopped chives
4 large or 8 medium portobello
   mushrooms
2 tablespoons extra virgin
   olive oil
1½ tablespoons white wine
   vinegar
2 teaspoons dijon mustard
1½ teaspoons maple syrup
1 handful basil leaves
1 handful flat-leaf parsley leaves
5 cups (200 g) mixed salad
   leaves

I love mushrooms, raw or cooked. I try to add them to as many meals as I can because they're cheap and they bulk up recipes. Also, they take on the flavour of the dish, so they always taste good! To make this a vegan meal, substitute the ricotta with silken tofu and the parmesan with ¼ cup (10 g) nutritional yeast flakes. For a gluten-free version, use gluten-free bread.

1   Preheat the oven to 180°C (350°F). Line a baking tray with baking paper.

2   Tear the sourdough into chunks and add it to a food processor along with the hazelnuts, parmesan and olive oil. Pulse to form chunky crumbs.

3   Place the spinach, ricotta, lemon juice, thyme and half the chives in a bowl and stir well to combine. Season with salt and freshly ground black pepper.

4   Place the mushrooms on the baking tray, stalk side up. Remove the stalks and season the mushroom cups with salt and pepper. Spoon the spinach mixture into the mushrooms, top with the sourdough crumbs and bake for 20–30 minutes (depending on size) or until the mushrooms are cooked and the crumbs are crisp and golden.

5   Meanwhile, blitz the extra virgin olive oil, vinegar, mustard, maple syrup, basil, parsley and remaining chives in a food processor until smooth. Season the dressing with salt and pepper, then pour it into a large bowl, add the salad leaves and toss together.

6   Served the stuffed mushrooms with the salad.

Curry chicken fried rice

Prep time: 20 minutes
Cook time: 15 minutes
Serves 4

---

3 teaspoons curry powder
2 tablespoons tamari or
   soy sauce
2 teaspoons fish sauce
2 teaspoons sesame oil
500 g (1 lb 2 oz) quick-cook
   long-grain rice (see Tip)
2 tablespoons peanut oil
3 eggs
500 g (1 lb 2 oz) boneless,
   skinless chicken thighs, sliced
1 bunch (about 150 g)
   broccolini, chopped
1 carrot, peeled, halved and
   thinly sliced
½ cup (65 g) frozen baby peas
1 tablespoon finely grated
   ginger
3 garlic cloves, crushed
150 g (5½ oz) snow peas
   (mange tout), halved
3 spring onions (scallions),
   chopped
1 handful coriander (cilantro)
   leaves

I've given traditional fried rice a big boost of green veggies!
Prawns or firm tofu would be wonderful substitutes for the
chicken – cook them in the same way as the chicken, but
remove them from the pan while you make the rest of the
dish and add them with the egg at the end.

1   Combine the curry powder, tamari, fish sauce and sesame
    oil in a small bowl. Set aside.

2   Gently massage the packets of rice to break up the rice inside.

3   Heat 1 teaspoon of the peanut oil in a wok or large frying pan
    over high heat. Whisk the eggs with 1½ tablespoons water
    and season with salt and freshly ground black pepper. Cook,
    stirring to scramble, for 1–2 minutes. Spoon the egg into a
    bowl and set aside.

4   Add the remaining peanut oil to the pan. Season the chicken
    with salt and pepper, then stir-fry for 5 minutes. Add the
    broccolini, carrot, peas, ginger and garlic and cook, stirring,
    for 2–3 minutes or until the chicken is cooked.

5   Stir in the rice and cook for 2 minutes. Add the curry mixture,
    stir well and cook for a few more minutes. Stir in the snow
    peas, spring onion and egg and cook for 1 minute. Serve the
    rice topped with the coriander.

Tip: You could use 3½ cups (650 g) of cold leftover cooked rice
instead of the quick-cook rice.

Chorizo and vongole baked risotto

Prep time: 10 minutes
Cook time: 40 minutes
Serves 4–6

1 tablespoon olive oil
1½ tablespoons (30 g) butter
2 leeks, pale parts only,
   thinly sliced
2 x 125 g (4½ oz) chorizo
   sausages, chopped
1 tablespoon thyme leaves
1¾ cups (400 g) arborio rice
1 cup (250 ml) white wine
4 cups (1 litre) vegetable stock
300 g (10½ oz) baby tomatoes,
   halved
2 zucchini (courgettes), grated
1 kg (2 lb 4 oz) vongole or
   small clams
Chopped flat-leaf parsley,
   to serve
Lemon wedges, to serve

If you're looking for a simple seafood dish that really hits the spot, this is it! If you can't find vongole or clams, use mussels instead. Or swap them for some firm fish or a different meat – perhaps bacon or Italian sausage.

1. Preheat the oven to 200°C (400°F).

2. Heat the oil and butter in a large ovenproof pan over medium–high heat. Cook the leek, chorizo and thyme for 10 minutes, stirring often.

3. Add the rice and stir to coat in the oil, then pour in the wine and let it boil for a couple of minutes until almost evaporated. Pour in the stock and bring to the boil. Stir in the tomatoes and zucchini and season with salt and freshly ground black pepper. Cover and bake for 25 minutes.

4. Remove the pan from the oven and stir in the vongole. Cover and return to the oven for a few minutes or until the rice is cooked and the vongole have opened. Serve sprinkled with chopped parsley, with the lemon wedges on the side.

Lemon and chive barramundi

Prep time: 5 minutes
Cook time: 20 minutes
Serves 2

2 barramundi or other firm
   white fish fillets, skin off
Juice of 1 lemon, plus extra
   lemon wedges to serve
2 tablespoons olive oil
1 tablespoon chives, finely
   chopped
Steamed rice or Chicken rice
   (page 181), to serve

This fish is lovely served with steamed rice or Chicken rice (page 181). You can also use salmon fillets, or swap the fish with chicken for a different protein source.

1   Preheat the oven to 180°C (350°F). Line a baking tray with baking paper and place the fish on the tray, skin side down. Sprinkle the fish with a generous pinch of salt and freshly ground black pepper. Bake for 20 minutes or until cooked to your liking.

2   Meanwhile, combine the lemon juice, olive oil and chives in a bowl. Season with salt and mix well.

3   Pour the lemon and chive mixture over the barramundi and serve immediately with the rice and lemon wedges.

Chicken enchiladas

Prep time: 30 minutes
Cook time: 35 minutes
Serves 4–6

Olive oil spray
3 cups (450 g) shredded
    barbecue chicken
400 g (14 oz) tin black beans,
    rinsed and drained
150 g (5½ oz) marinated red
    capsicum (pepper), chopped
    (page 184)
2½ cups (625 ml) tomato
    passata (puréed tomatoes)
1½ cups (150 g) grated cheddar
    cheese
1½ cups (190 g) grated
    mozzarella cheese
6 spring onions (scallions),
    chopped
1 bunch coriander (cilantro),
    chopped
2 teaspoons sweet paprika
2 teaspoons ground cumin
6 wholegrain tortillas
½ iceberg lettuce, shredded
3 tomatoes, seeded and diced
1 green capsicum (pepper),
    diced
1 avocado, diced
Juice of 1 lime
1 tablespoon extra virgin olive oil
Reduced-fat sour cream,
    to serve

Enchiladas are a great dish to make and freeze, ready to heat when you don't want to cook. Make this a gluten-free meal by using gluten-free tortillas. For a vegetarian version, replace the chicken with extra beans.

1   Preheat the oven to 180°C (350°F). Line a 22 cm (8½ inch) round cake tin with baking paper and spray with olive oil.

2   Combine the chicken, black beans, marinated capsicum, 2 cups (500 ml) of the passata, two-thirds of the grated cheeses, two-thirds of the spring onion, half the coriander and the paprika and cumin in a large bowl and season with salt and freshly ground black pepper.

3   Trim 1 cm (½ inch) off the top and bottom of the tortillas to create flat edges. Divide the chicken mixture among the tortillas, spreading it to cover the whole surface, then roll up so that the cut edges are at the top and bottom.

4   Cut each enchilada into thirds and stand them upright in the lined tin. Top with the remaining passata and grated cheeses. Cover the tin with foil and bake for 25 minutes. Remove the foil and bake for another 10 minutes or until the enchiladas are golden.

5   Meanwhile, combine the lettuce, tomato, green capsicum, avocado, remaining coriander and spring onion in a large bowl. Add the lime juice and olive oil, season with salt and pepper and toss well.

6   Serve the enchiladas with sour cream and the salsa salad.

Tip: To line the tin, scrunch up a large square of baking paper, then smooth it out and press it into the tin. This will also assist in lifting the enchiladas out of the tin.

Baked cauliflower and prawn biryani

Prep time: 20 minutes
Cook time: 35 minutes
Serves 4

---

1 tablespoon finely grated
   ginger
4 garlic cloves, crushed
2 teaspoons curry powder
2 teaspoons garam masala
½ teaspoon chilli powder
½ cup (130 g) Greek-style
   yoghurt
24 raw prawns, peeled and
   deveined, tails on
2 cups (500 ml) vegetable
   stock
1 tablespoon honey
½ teaspoon ground turmeric
⅔ cup (60 g) crispy fried
   shallots, plus extra to serve
6 cups (780 g) cauliflower rice
300 g (10½ oz) green beans,
   topped and tailed
2 cinnamon sticks
6 cardamom pods, bruised
Coriander (cilantro) leaves,
   to serve

I love this biryani so much! Cauliflower and prawns are a fabulous combo and together they make for a hearty and tasty meal. You can buy ready-made cauliflower rice, but it's easy to make your own by putting the cauliflower florets in a food processor and pulsing until it reaches the consistency of rice. For a dairy-free dish, replace the Greek yoghurt with coconut yoghurt.

1 Preheat the oven to 220°C (425°F).

2 Combine the ginger, garlic, curry powder, garam masala, chilli powder and some salt in a bowl. Spoon half of the spice mix into an ovenproof dish, about 25 x 30 cm (10 x 12 inches).

3 Stir the yoghurt into the remaining spice mix. Add the prawns and toss to coat, then set aside.

4 Add the stock, honey and turmeric to the spice mix in the ovenproof dish and stir well to combine. Add the fried shallots, cauliflower rice, beans, cinnamon sticks and cardamom pods and stir to combine. Cover with foil and bake for 25 minutes.

5 Remove the foil and place the prawns on top of the cauliflower mixture. Bake for another 10 minutes or until the prawns are cooked through.

6 Serve the biryani sprinkled with coriander leaves and extra fried shallots.

Chicken rice

Prep time: 5 minutes
Cook time: 20 minutes
Serves 4–6 as a side

1 tablespoon (20 g) butter
½ small brown onion, diced
3 allspice berries
3 cloves
1 cup (200 g) basmati rice,
    rinsed
2 cups (500 ml) chicken stock

This chicken rice was a creation that my mum came up with when we wouldn't eat 'boring' rice, as we'd call it! I make this as a side dish with any dinner – it suits everything. Kids love it, and it's perfect for meal prep.

1   In a small saucepan with a lid, heat the butter over medium heat and stir until melted. Add the onion, allspice and cloves and cook for 3 minutes or until the onion is translucent.

2   Stir in the rice, add the stock and cover the pan. Bring to the boil, then turn down to a simmer and put a timer on for 15 minutes.

3   When the timer goes off, remove the pan from the heat and discard the allspice and cloves. Fluff with a fork for extra-fluffy rice.

Pickled zucchini

Prep time: 10 minutes,
    plus draining
Cook time: 10 minutes
Serves 10 as a side

---

5 white zucchini (courgettes)
2 tablespoons salt
1 cup (250 ml) white vinegar
2–3 garlic cloves, crushed
1 teaspoon dried oregano
2 cups (500 ml) neutral-
    flavoured oil, or as needed

I use these zucchini as a snack, chopped in salads, on top of toast or just as a side dish to a beautiful dinner – they go well with so many dishes. You can use green zucchini, but the white ones are crunchier.

1   Cut the zucchini lengthways into quarters and scoop out the seeds (you can use them in the Carrot, cauliflower and corn fritters on page 52). Slice the zucchini into long strips, place them in a colander and sprinkle with the salt. Leave to drain over a bowl in the fridge for 5–6 hours to extract as much liquid as possible.

2   Bring the vinegar and 2 cups (500 ml) water to the boil in a deep saucepan. Add the zucchini and boil for 3–4 minutes or until slightly tender but still crisp in the centre. Drain the zucchini and leave to cool.

3   Add the zucchini to a jar and top with the garlic, oregano and enough of the oil to completely cover the zucchini. Seal and store in the fridge for up to 6 weeks.

Tips: This might seem like a lot of salt, but don't stress! The salt is used to draw out the excess liquid in the zucchini, so that they keep that crunch after you boil them.

If you want to increase the quantity, use 1 part vinegar to 2 parts water for the pickling liquid.

Don't use olive oil for this recipe as it will solidify in the fridge.

Marinated capsicum

Prep time: 10 minutes,
   plus 15 minutes standing
Cook time: 10 minutes
Serves 10 as a side

---

4 large red capsicums (peppers)
½ cup (125 ml) extra virgin
   olive oil
½ cup (125 ml) neutral-
   flavoured oil, or as needed
3 garlic cloves, thinly sliced
½ teaspoon salt

This capsicum can be used in many different ways – use it to add a little zing to your salads or serve it as a side dish. I love it on toast with a little taramasalata. Thanks for the recipe, Yiayia!

1   Preheat the grill to high (200°C/400°F). Line a baking tray with baking paper.

2   Cut the capsicums in half lengthways and remove the seeds and membrane. Place the capsicum halves on the baking tray, skin side up, and splash a little olive oil over them. Grill for 10 minutes or until the skins have begun to blacken.

3   Transfer the capsicum halves to a plastic bag and seal the bag with a knot, ensuring no air can escape. Leave to steam for 15 minutes, then take the capsicum out of the bag and remove the skin by peeling it from one edge to the other.

4   Place the capsicum in a container and pour in enough of the neutral-flavoured oil to completely cover it. (Don't use olive oil as it will solidify in the fridge.) Gently stir in the garlic and salt. Seal and store the capsicum in the fridge for up to 3 months, topping up the oil as needed so that the capsicum is completely covered. You can also freeze the marinated capsicum in the oil for up to a year.

Chimichurri

Prep time: 10 minutes
Cook time: Nil
Makes about 1 cup

1 bunch flat-leaf parsley,
　　leaves picked
1 bunch coriander (cilantro)
1 spring onion (scallion), cut
　　into 2 cm (¾ inch) lengths
1 long red chilli, seeded and
　　finely chopped
2 garlic cloves, sliced
½ cup (125 ml) mild-flavoured
　　olive oil
Juice of ½ lemon, or as needed
1 teaspoon sweet paprika

This has become one of my favourite dressings. I love it over a juicy steak or a piece of baked salmon – any protein goes! If you like a little more heat, add a spicier chilli or some cayenne pepper.

1　Blitz the parsley, coriander, spring onion, chilli and garlic in a food processor until finely chopped. You may need to stop and scrape down the side of the bowl to ensure the herbs are all chopped.

2　Add the olive oil, lemon juice and paprika and season with salt and freshly ground black pepper. Blitz until combined. Taste and adjust the seasoning, adding more lemon juice or salt if needed.

3　Store the chimichurri in the fridge for up to 3 days or freeze it in ice-cube trays and thaw it in the fridge or microwave when needed.

Papou's secret lemon barbecue dressing

Prep time: 5 minutes
Cook time: Nil
Makes about ½ cup

---

1 lemon, halved
¼ cup (60 ml) olive oil
1 garlic clove, crushed
1 teaspoon dried oregano
½ teaspoon salt
½ teaspoon freshly ground
   black pepper

This dressing is perfect on any protein, especially chicken and seafood, and an absolute winner in our home. It can be added to meat while it's cooking on the barbecue, or just as it comes off to really lock in the flavour. The dressing can be frozen for up to 6 months and thawed whenever you're barbecuing.

1   Juice the lemon, reserving one of the halves for basting. Add the lemon juice, olive oil, garlic, oregano, salt and pepper to a small bowl and mix to combine.

2   Pierce the skin of the reserved lemon half with a fork, then dip the lemon into the dressing and use it to brush the dressing onto the meat while it's barbecuing. (This is the traditional method – you could use a basting brush, but where's the fun in that?)

Olive sprinkle

Prep time: 5 minutes
Cook time: 1 hour 20 minutes
Makes about 1½ cups

2 cups (360 g) kalamata olives,
  pitted

This is perfect to throw into a salad, or sprinkle over some protein or a pasta dish for a little salty bite. I use it to flavour my Rosemary and olive flatbreads (see page 230).

1   Put the olives in the basket of an air fryer. Close the air fryer and turn it to 180°C (350°F) for 50 minutes. Alternatively, preheat the oven to 180°C (350°F) and cook the olives on a baking tray lined with baking paper for 1 hour 20 minutes or until they have dried out.

2   Leave the olives to cool slightly, and then grab a sharp knife and start chopping! Keep going until the olives are finely diced. (I don't recommend using a food processor in case it heats the olives and makes them mushy, and in case there's a wandering pip in the olives – this can ruin the whole sprinkle.)

3   Store the olive sprinkle in a jar or an airtight container for up to 6 weeks.

Briam veggies

Prep time: 10 minutes
Cook time: 40 minutes
Serves 6 as a side

⅓ cup (80 ml) olive oil
¼ cup (60 g) tomato paste
   (concentrated purée)
2 tablespoons finely chopped
   flat-leaf parsley
3 garlic cloves, thinly sliced
2 carrots
2 zucchini (courgettes)
1 large eggplant (aubergine)
1 large brown onion
10 baby potatoes

I have to thank Yiayia Itsines for this recipe for Greek tomato vegetables. It's a delicious side dish that's perfect served with a lovely cut of protein and a salad.

1   Preheat the oven to 180°C (350°F). Line a large roasting tin with baking paper.

2   Combine the olive oil, tomato paste, parsley and garlic in a bowl. Season with salt and freshly ground black pepper and mix well.

3   Slice the carrots, zucchini and eggplant into 2 cm (¾ inch) rounds. Cut the eggplant rounds into quarters, cut the onion into wedges and halve the baby potatoes.

4   Combine all of the veggies in a large bowl and pour in the tomato mixture. Mix to coat well, ensuring the veggies are completely covered.

5   Tip the veggies into the roasting tin and spread out evenly. Roast in the oven for 40 minutes or until the potato and carrot are cooked through.

The ENTER~

Epic meals that will 'wow' your guests (with minimal effort)

4

~TAIN ER

THE
ENTERTAINER

Spicy beef roast

Prep time: 20 minutes
Cook time: 4¼ hours
Serves 4–6

1–2 kg (2 lb 4 oz–4 lb 8 oz)
   beef bolar blade roast
3–4 garlic cloves, crushed
Olive oil, for cooking
1 cup (250 ml) beef stock
½ cup (125 ml) tomato passata
   (puréed tomatoes)
2 tablespoons dijon mustard
2 carrots, peeled and quartered
   lengthways
2 potatoes, peeled and
   quartered
2 brown onions, quartered
1 teaspoon cornflour
   (cornstarch)

DRY RUB
2 tablespoons fennel seeds
2–4 teaspoons chilli flakes,
   or to taste
1 tablespoon smoked paprika
1 tablespoon salt
2 teaspoons freshly ground
   black pepper
2 teaspoons dried oregano
1 teaspoon cumin seeds
1 teaspoon ground turmeric

Roasts make me so happy because they remind me of family dinners. In winter, we cook a beef or lamb roast every Sunday with the family – it's such a special time. This was a recipe I made when it was my turn to make dinner!

1 Preheat the oven to 150°C (300°F).

2 Prepare the dry rub by combining all of the ingredients in a small bowl.

3 Trim the excess fat from the bolar roast and use a small knife to cut deep pockets into both sides of the meat. Push the crushed garlic into the pockets. Sprinkle the dry rub over the beef to completely coat it.

4 Heat the olive oil in a large frying pan over medium heat and sear the beef on all sides.

5 Put the stock, passata and mustard in a small bowl and mix well to combine.

6 Add the carrot, potato and onion pieces to a large, deep ovenproof saucepan. Sit the beef on top of the vegetables and pour the stock mixture over the top. Cover and roast in the oven for 4 hours.

7 Remove the beef and vegetables from the pan and set aside. Rest the beef for 10 minutes before slicing.

8 Place the pan on the stove over medium–high heat. Mix the cornflour with 1 teaspoon water, stir into the pan juices and cook for 5–8 minutes or until thickened.

9 Slice the beef and serve it with the thickened pan juices and vegetables.

Tips: You can pour the pan juices straight over the roast without thickening them.

If you're serving a crowd, you can easily double the vegetables or add a side of Balsamic pumpkin (page 229) or one of the cauliflower or broccoli dishes on pages 44–45.

Szechuan pepper salmon

Prep time: 20 minutes
Cook time: 25 minutes
Serves 4

1¼ cups (250 g) jasmine rice, rinsed
400 ml (14 fl oz) reduced-fat coconut milk
1 cup (250 ml) vegetable stock
2 corncobs, kernels removed
4 pak choy, quartered
1 tablespoon Szechuan peppercorns (see Tip)
2 teaspoons sea salt flakes
¼ teaspoon ground white pepper
2 teaspoons brown sugar
750 g (1 lb 10 oz) boneless, skinless salmon
2 teaspoons peanut oil
3 spring onions (scallions), sliced
½ cup (80 g) roasted cashews, roughly chopped
1 handful coriander (cilantro) leaves

This salmon is incredible. If you don't usually enjoy fish, try cooking this to ease yourself into it. Use firm tofu in place of the salmon for a fantastic vegan dish.

1   Add the rice, coconut milk, stock and a pinch of salt to a saucepan and stir to combine. Bring to the boil over high heat, then reduce the heat to low, cover and cook for 8 minutes. Stir in the corn and top with the pak choy, cover and cook for 7–10 minutes or until the rice and vegetables are cooked.

2   Meanwhile, toast the Szechuan peppercorns in a large frying pan over medium–high heat for a few minutes until fragrant. Tip into a mortar and finely grind with the pestle (or use an electric spice grinder).

3   Add the sea salt flakes, white pepper, brown sugar and ground Szechuan pepper to a bowl and stir to combine.

4   Cut the salmon into 3 cm (1¼ inch) cubes, add it to the spice mix and toss to coat.

5   Return the frying pan to high heat and add the peanut oil. Cook the salmon, turning to cook on all sides, for 5 minutes or until cooked to your liking.

6   Spoon the rice and pak choy into serving bowls and top with the salmon, spring onion, cashews and coriander.

Tip: Szechuan peppercorns are sold in Asian grocery stores.

Sage and cider roast pork with braised fennel and polenta

Prep time: 20 minutes, plus
overnight resting
Cook time: 1¼ hours
Serves 6

1.5 kg (3 lb 5 oz) boneless rolled
    pork loin roast
2 teaspoons olive oil
1 bunch sage, leaves picked
1 garlic bulb, halved
1⅓ cups (330 ml) alcoholic
    apple cider
4 cups (1 litre) chicken stock
3 baby fennel bulbs, quartered
1½ cups (285 g) polenta
2½ tablespoons (50 g) butter
1½ cups (200 g) frozen baby
    peas
3 cups (150 g) baby spinach

I love roast pork and this one is perfect for a special weekend meal when you have friends coming for dinner. Serve it with some extra veggies on the side for a perfect meal.

1   Place the pork on a tray. Dry the rind with paper towel and then score it with a small sharp knife. Rub the rind generously with salt and refrigerate overnight, uncovered.

2   Remove the pork from the fridge 1 hour before cooking. Preheat the oven to 250°C (500°F).

3   Wipe the liquid off the pork rind, then rub it with the olive oil and a little more salt. Place the pork in a large roasting tin, rind side up, with the sage and garlic. Pour in the cider and 1½ cups (375 ml) of the stock (or enough so that it comes up the side of the pork but doesn't touch the rind). Roast for 20 minutes. Remove the pork from the oven and reduce the heat to 180°C (350°F). Place the fennel pieces around the pork and season with salt and freshly ground black pepper. Roast for 45 minutes or until the pork is cooked and the fennel is tender.

4   When the pork is almost ready, pour the remaining stock and 2 cups (500 ml) water into a large saucepan and bring to a simmer over medium–high heat. Add the polenta in a steady stream, whisking constantly. Reduce the heat to low and cook for a few minutes until soft (add a little extra water if it's too thick). Add the butter, then stir in the peas and spinach and cook for 5 minutes. Season with salt and pepper.

5   Remove the pork and fennel from the tin and set aside to rest before slicing. Place the roasting tin over high heat and bring the liquid to the boil. Mash the garlic with a fork and continue boiling for a few minutes or until the sauce has reduced to about 1 cup (250 ml). Strain the sauce through a sieve.

6   Spoon the polenta onto serving plates, add the sliced pork and fennel and spoon the sauce over the top.

Tip: If your crackling isn't crisp enough, pop it under a hot grill.

Herb-crusted lamb rack on scalloped sweet potato

Prep time: 30 minutes
Cook time: 1 hour
Serves 6

---

2 French-trimmed lamb racks
1.2 kg (2 lb 11 oz) sweet potato
1 red onion, thinly sliced
1⅓ cups (135 g) finely grated
   parmesan cheese
1½ tablespoons thyme leaves
⅔ cup (170 ml) vegetable stock
1½ tablespoons (30 g) butter
⅓ cup (45 g) pistachio kernels
1 bunch chives, roughly chopped
1 handful flat-leaf parsley leaves
1 handful mint leaves
1 rosemary stalk, leaves picked
1 cup (60 g) panko breadcrumbs
2 tablespoons olive oil, plus
   extra for greasing
1 tablespoon dijon mustard
1 egg white

This herb-crusted lamb rack looks incredible, so if you have some guests you'd like to wow at dinnertime, pick this one!

1   Preheat the oven to 200°C (400°F). Take the lamb racks out of the fridge.

2   Peel and slice the sweet potato, cutting it into 2 mm (1/16 inch) slices. Layer the sweet potato and onion slices in an ovenproof dish, scattering the parmesan, thyme, salt and freshly ground black pepper over each layer. Pour the stock over the top and dot with the butter. Cover with foil and bake for 35 minutes.

3   Meanwhile, add the pistachios, chives, parsley, mint, rosemary, breadcrumbs and olive oil to a food processor with some salt and pepper and blitz until finely chopped. Tip the herb crumbs into a large bowl.

4   Line a baking tray with baking paper and rub or spray it with olive oil.

5   Season the lamb racks with some salt and pepper. Whisk the mustard with the egg white. Generously brush the mixture over the underside of one of the lamb racks and press it into the herb crumbs. Brush the top and sides of the lamb with the mustard mixture and press it into the herb crumbs. Place on the oiled tray and repeat with the remaining lamb rack.

6   Remove the foil from the sweet potato and return it to the oven along with the lamb racks. Roast the lamb racks for 25 minutes for medium or until cooked to your liking.

7   Rest the lamb racks for 10 minutes before slicing them into portions. Serve with the scalloped sweet potato.

Tip: Use a mandolin or food processor to make slicing the sweet potato and onion easy.

Cattleman's cutlet
with roast vegetables

Prep time: 15 minutes, plus
   1 hour standing
Cook time: 45 minutes
Serves 2

---

700 g (1 lb 9 oz) thick-cut
   rib eye on the bone
¼ cup (60 ml) olive oil
1½ tablespoons thyme leaves
5 garlic cloves, crushed
350 g (12 oz) kent pumpkin
   (squash), cut into wedges
250 g (9 oz) baby potatoes,
   quartered
150 g (5½ oz) brussels sprouts,
   halved
100 g (3½ oz) Swiss brown
   mushrooms
¼ cup (60 ml) Marsala
¾ cup (185 ml) beef stock
2 tablespoons single (pure)
   cream
1 tablespoon dijon mustard
1 handful chopped flat-leaf
   parsley, to serve

My extended family are one of those 'where's the meat?' families (think *My Big Fat Greek Wedding!*), and this is definitely meaty! Rib eye on the bone is also known as prime rib or a cattleman's cutlet. You'll need a 5–6 cm (2–2½ inch) thick piece.

1 Take the rib eye out of the fridge an hour before cooking (you'll get a more evenly cooked piece of meat). Preheat the oven to 200°C (400°F).

2 Heat 1 tablespoon of the olive oil in a large ovenproof frying pan over high heat. Season the rib eye with salt and freshly ground black pepper and place in the pan for a few minutes to brown well on one side.

3 Meanwhile, stir together the remaining oil, thyme and half the garlic in a large bowl. Add the vegetables and toss well to coat, then season with salt and pepper.

4 Remove the pan from the heat, turn the rib eye over and arrange the vegetables evenly around the sides. Place in the oven and cook for 25 minutes for a medium result or until cooked to your liking. Rest the rib eye on a board, loosely covered with foil, before slicing.

5 While the meat is resting, increase the oven to 240°C (475°F). Toss the vegetables in the pan juices and cook for another 10 minutes or until golden and tender. Divide the vegetables between serving plates.

6 Place the frying pan over high heat. Deglaze the pan with the Marsala and let it bubble away for 1 minute, then add the remaining garlic, stock, cream, mustard, any resting juices and a generous amount of pepper. Boil for a few minutes until the sauce has reduced and thickened slightly. Taste and season with salt, if needed.

7 Serve the steak cut into thick slices, drizzled with the sauce and sprinkled with the parsley, with the roasted vegetables on the side.

Roast lamb with fasolakia lathera

Prep time: 25 minutes
Cook time: 1 hour 20 minutes
Serves 6–8

½ cup (125 ml) extra virgin
   olive oil
Finely grated zest and juice
   of 1 lemon
2 tablespoons dried oregano
6 garlic cloves, crushed
1.8 kg (4 lb) butterflied lamb leg
1 large brown onion, chopped
1½ teaspoons ground cumin
750 g (1 lb 10 oz) green beans
600 g (1 lb 5 oz) baby potatoes,
   cut into 1 cm (½ inch) slices
400 g (14 oz) tin diced
   tomatoes
2 bay leaves
200 g (7 oz) Greek feta cheese,
   crumbled
1 handful chopped flat-leaf
   parsley

Fasolakia is another Yiayia gem! In Greek, 'fasolakia' is braised beans. It's one of my yiayia's favourite dishes to make because she grows her own beans (of course). I grew up eating this dish, so it's a very special recipe to me.

1 Preheat the oven to 180°C (350°F).

2 Combine 2 tablespoons of the olive oil with the lemon zest, lemon juice, oregano, garlic and some salt and freshly ground black pepper in a large bowl. Add the lamb and coat well in the marinade.

3 Heat a large ovenproof frying pan over medium–high heat. Sear the lamb, skin side down, for 5 minutes or until golden. Transfer the lamb to a plate and set aside to come to room temperature while you prepare the beans.

4 Heat the remaining olive oil in the same pan, add the onion with a generous pinch of salt and cook for a few minutes. Add the cumin and cook for 1 minute, then add the beans and potatoes and stir to coat in the oil.

5 Add the tomatoes, bay leaves and ⅔ cup (170 ml) water, then season with salt and pepper. Bring to a simmer, then remove from the heat, cover and transfer to the oven to cook for 30 minutes.

6 Stir the vegetables, then place the lamb on top and roast, uncovered, for about 40 minutes for medium (depending on the thickness of the lamb) or until cooked to your liking. Rest the lamb before slicing.

7 Sprinkle the beans and potatoes with the feta and parsley and serve with the sliced lamb.

Chicken saagwala with curried crushed potatoes

Prep time: 25 minutes
Cook time: 30 minutes
Serves 4

---

800 g (1 lb 12 oz) baby potatoes
⅓ cup (65 g) ghee
2 brown onions, chopped
4 garlic cloves, crushed
1 tablespoon finely grated
　ginger
1 green chilli, chopped
1 tablespoon ground coriander
3 teaspoons ground cumin
3 teaspoons garam masala
¼ teaspoon ground turmeric
2 tomatoes, chopped
5 cups (250 g) baby spinach
½ cup (125 ml) vegetable stock
800 g (1 lb 12 oz) skinless,
　boneless chicken thighs,
　halved or quartered if large
½ cup (125 ml) coconut milk
1 tablespoon honey
1 tablespoon mustard seeds
1½ teaspoons curry powder
1 handful coriander (cilantro),
　chopped

Curried crushed potatoes ... they taste as good as they sound! Although ghee is made from butter, it is considered to be dairy free because the lactose and casein have been separated out.

1　Bring a large saucepan of salted water to the boil. Cook the potatoes for 15–20 minutes or until tender, then drain and set aside.

2　Meanwhile, heat half the ghee in a large saucepan over medium–high heat. Cook the onion with a generous pinch of salt for 6–8 minutes or until soft. Transfer half the onion to a bowl and set aside.

3　Add the garlic, ginger, chilli, ground coriander, cumin, garam masala and turmeric to the onion in the pan and cook for a couple of minutes or until fragrant. Stir in the tomato, spinach and stock and cook until the spinach has just wilted.

4　Spoon the mixture into a blender and blend until smooth. Season with salt and freshly ground black pepper.

5　Return the sauce to the pan and add the chicken, coconut milk and honey. Bring to a simmer, then reduce the heat to low and gently simmer for 10–15 minutes or until the chicken is cooked through.

6　Meanwhile, heat the remaining ghee in a frying pan over medium–high heat. Add the mustard seeds and cook for a couple of minutes until they pop and crackle. Add the curry powder and reserved onion and cook for 1 minute. Add the potatoes and lightly crush them with a fork to break them up (but don't mash them). Stir to coat in the spices and season with salt and pepper.

7　Serve the potatoes with the chicken saagwala, sprinkled with the chopped coriander.

Slow-cooked Mexican beef with elote salad

Prep time: 20 minutes,
    plus 1 hour marinating
Cook time: 5½ hours
Serves 6–8

1.5 kg (3 lb 5 oz) beef brisket
6 corncobs, husks removed
¼ cup (70 g) Greek-style
    yoghurt
¼ cup (60 g) whole egg
    mayonnaise
2 tablespoons lime juice
1 garlic clove, crushed
2 jalapeño chillies, seeded
    and finely chopped
4 spring onions (scallions),
    chopped
2 bunches coriander (cilantro),
    chopped
200 g (7 oz) Greek feta cheese,
    crumbled
Mini tortillas, to serve

SPICE MIX
¼ cup (60 ml) olive oil
1 tablespoon chipotle in adobo
    sauce, finely chopped
3 teaspoons honey
3 teaspoons onion powder
3 teaspoons ground coriander
2 teaspoons garlic powder
2 teaspoons ground cumin
2 teaspoons smoked paprika
2 teaspoons salt

Anything slow cooked is a favourite of mine, and with the Mexican-inspired spices, this brisket is a winner. You can marinate it the night before for extra flavour – remove it from the fridge 1 hour before cooking to bring it to room temperature. Use any leftover brisket in wraps or chop it up and add it to nachos.

1   Combine the spice mix ingredients in a small bowl.

2   Dry the brisket with paper towel and place it on a wire rack sitting in a roasting tin. Rub the spice mix all over the brisket. Set aside for 1 hour to marinate and come to room temperature.

3   Preheat the oven to 140°C (275°F).

4   Pour enough water into the roasting tin to come 1 cm (½ inch) up the sides without touching the meat on the rack. Cover with foil and bake for 5 hours.

5   Remove the foil and cook for a further 30 minutes to brown the meat. Remove from the oven, loosely cover with foil and set aside to rest before slicing.

6   Meanwhile, grill the corn on a barbecue or chargrill pan over medium–high heat, turning until lightly charred on all sides, for about 8–10 minutes. Set aside to cool, then cut off the kernels.

7   Mix the yoghurt, mayonnaise, lime juice, crushed garlic and chopped jalapeños together in a large bowl. Add the corn, spring onion and most of the coriander and feta and toss well to combine. Season with salt and freshly ground black pepper.

8   Serve the salad with the sliced brisket and mini tortillas, topped with the remaining feta and coriander.

Beef cheek and mushroom ragu

Prep time: 15 minutes
Cook time: 3 hours 20 minutes
Serves 6–8

20 g (¾ oz) dried porcini
   mushrooms
1 cup (250 ml) boiling water
1½ tablespoons olive oil
1 kg (2 lb 4 oz) beef cheeks,
   halved
1 carrot, peeled and roughly
   chopped
2 celery stalks, roughly chopped
1 large brown onion, roughly
   chopped
4 garlic cloves, peeled
1 tablespoon dried oregano
350 g (12 oz) Swiss brown
   mushrooms, halved or
   quartered if large
1 cup (250 ml) shiraz
1 cup (250 ml) tomato passata
   (puréed tomatoes)
1 cup (250 ml) beef stock
2 tablespoons maple syrup
2 bay leaves
800 g (1 lb 12 oz) rigatoni pasta
1 bunch basil, leaves picked
Grated parmesan cheese,
   to serve

I love to have a batch of ragu in the freezer, ready for a quick pasta dinner or lasagne filling, so I recommend making this in bulk. Blitzing the vegetables in a food processor is easier and faster than chopping them and it also makes the sauce thicker, so there's no need to reduce the braising liquid at the end.

1   Preheat the oven to 150°C (300°F).

2   Soak the porcini mushrooms in the boiling water for 10 minutes, then drain, reserving the soaking liquid.

3   Meanwhile, heat the olive oil in a large ovenproof saucepan over medium–high heat. Season the beef cheeks with salt and freshly ground black pepper and brown well on both sides. Remove from the pan and set aside.

4   Blitz the carrot, celery, onion, garlic, oregano and porcini in a food processor until finely chopped. Add to the pan along with the Swiss brown mushrooms and cook for 8–10 minutes or until beginning to colour.

5   Add the wine, passata, stock, maple syrup and bay leaves. Season with salt and freshly ground black pepper and add the porcini soaking liquid, leaving behind any sediment that has settled to the bottom. Return the beef to the pan and bring to a simmer. Cover and cook in the oven for 3 hours or until the beef is meltingly tender.

6   About 20 minutes before the beef is cooked, bring a large saucepan of salted water to the boil. Add the pasta and cook according to the packet instructions, then drain well.

7   Remove the bay leaves and beef from the braising liquid. Shred the beef using two forks, then stir it through the sauce along with the basil. Season with salt and pepper. Stir the ragu through the pasta and serve topped with parmesan cheese.

Beef and veggie shepherd's pie

Prep time: 20 minutes
Cook time: 45 minutes
Serves 4

---

1 zucchini (courgette)
1 carrot
1 large brown onion
5 button mushrooms
1 kg (2 lb 4 oz) white potatoes,
    peeled and chopped
1 tablespoon olive oil
550 g (1 lb 4 oz) lean beef
    mince
3 garlic cloves, crushed
1 red chilli, seeded and sliced
1 cup (250 ml) chicken stock,
    or as needed
2 tablespoons tomato paste
    (concentrated purée)
2 tablespoons Worcestershire
    sauce
2 tablespoons (40 g) butter
½ teaspoon sweet paprika

This yummy pie is hearty comfort food at its best. You can also freeze it, then throw it in the oven when you get home late from work.

1 Preheat the oven to 180°C (350°F).

2 Grate the zucchini, then squeeze to remove as much liquid as possible. Grate the carrot, dice the onion and slice the button mushrooms.

3 Bring a large saucepan of water to the boil. Add the chopped potatoes and boil for 20 minutes or until cooked through.

4 Meanwhile, heat the oil in a deep saucepan over medium–high heat. Brown the beef mince, breaking it up into smaller pieces as it cooks. Add the onion and garlic and cook for 3 minutes. Add the zucchini, carrot, mushrooms and chilli. Cook, stirring, for 5–6 minutes or until the beef is cooked through. Stir in the stock, tomato paste and Worcestershire sauce and season with salt and freshly ground black pepper, adding a little more stock if the mixture looks dry. Cook for 3–4 minutes.

5 While the filling is cooking, drain the potatoes and transfer them to a large bowl. Mash until smooth, then add the butter. Season with salt and pepper and mix thoroughly.

6 Pour the filling into a deep ovenproof dish and level the top. Using a meat-baller or an ice-cream scoop, scoop the potato on top of the filling to completely cover it. Sprinkle the paprika over the potato and bake for 25 minutes or until the pie is lightly brown on top.

Five-spice chicken with sugar snap pea pilaf

Prep time: 15 minutes
Cook time: 40 minutes
Serves 4

1.4 kg (3 lb 2 oz) butterflied
  chicken (see Tip)
2 tablespoons peanut oil
1 tablespoon Chinese five-spice
  powder
¼ teaspoon cayenne pepper
2 French shallots, finely
  chopped
1½ cups (300 g) jasmine rice
300 g (10½ oz) sugar snap peas
2 Lebanese (short) cucumbers,
  seeded and julienned
2 spring onions (scallions),
  julienned
1 handful coriander (cilantro)
⅓ cup (50 g) chopped peanuts

Did someone say 'delicious'? I love a quick-and-easy pilaf, and this one is full of flavour that the family will absolutely love.

1 Preheat the oven to 200°C (400°F).

2 Place the chicken on a baking tray lined with baking paper. Combine 1½ tablespoons of the peanut oil with the five-spice powder, cayenne pepper and some salt and freshly ground black pepper. Rub the spiced oil all over the chicken.

3 Roast the chicken, skin side up, for 40 minutes or until the skin is crisp and the chicken is cooked through. Set aside to rest for 5 minutes.

4 While the chicken is roasting, heat the remaining peanut oil in a saucepan over medium–high heat. Cook the shallots with a generous pinch of salt for a couple of minutes or until translucent. Stir in the rice and cook for a couple of minutes, then pour in 2¼ cups (560 ml) water. Bring to the boil, then reduce the heat to low, cover and cook for 10 minutes. When the rice is almost cooked, place the sugar snap peas on top, cover and cook for a few minutes or until the rice is tender.

5 Cut the chicken into portions and place it on top of the pilaf, along with the cucumber, spring onion, coriander and peanuts. Drizzle any resting juices over the top.

Tip: If you can't buy your chicken butterflied, you can do it yourself by placing a whole chicken on a board, breast side down. Use kitchen scissors to cut along either side of the backbone to remove it. Discard the backbone, open out the chicken and turn it over, then push down on the breastbone to flatten.

Red curry fish

Prep time: 10 minutes
Cook time: 30 minutes
Serves 4–6

½ cup (125 g) red curry paste
½ cup (125 ml) coconut milk
1 kg (2 lb 4 oz) side of boneless,
  skinless firm white fish, such
  as snapper
2 bunches (about 300 g)
  asparagus
2 bunches (about 480 g)
  Chinese broccoli
⅔ cup (170 ml) vegetable stock
3 spring onions (scallions),
  julienned
1 bunch coriander (cilantro),
  leaves picked
⅓ cup (50 g) chopped peanuts
Steamed rice, to serve
Lime wedges, to serve

A simple red curry is a great option to cook before you head off to work – put it in the slow cooker and come home to a house smelling beautiful and dinner ready to serve. This can be slow cooked for 8 hours on low or 4 hours on high.

1 Preheat the oven to 200°C (400°F). Line an ovenproof dish with baking paper.

2 Combine the curry paste and coconut milk in a small bowl. Rub half of the mixture over the underside of the fish.

3 Trim the asparagus and Chinese broccoli and place in the lined dish to make a bed for the fish. Pour in the stock, then add the fish. Pour the remaining curry mixture over the fish and tuck the tail end underneath so the fish has the same thickness throughout. Roast for 25–30 minutes or until the fish is just cooked.

4 Scatter the spring onion, coriander and peanuts over the fish and serve with steamed rice and lime wedges.

Lamb shank, eggplant and cauliflower curry

Prep time: 30 minutes
Cook time: 2¾ hours
Serves 4

Slow-cooked lamb shanks are great for a simple weekend meal. You can spend 30 minutes preparing this in the morning, then leave it to cook for a scrumptious dinner. Replace the ghee with oil if you prefer.

2 tablespoons ghee
4 lamb shanks
1 brown onion, chopped
1 eggplant (aubergine), cut into
    3 cm (1¼ inch) cubes
1 tablespoon grated ginger
3 garlic cloves, crushed
1½ tablespoons garam masala
3 teaspoons ground coriander
1 teaspoon ground cumin
1 teaspoon ground turmeric
400 g (14 oz) tin diced tomatoes
2 cups (500 ml) chicken stock
1 cup (250 ml) coconut milk
400 g (14 oz) tin chickpeas,
    rinsed and drained
2 tablespoons honey
½ cauliflower, cut into florets

GARLIC AND LEMON
NAAN
2 cups (300 g) wholemeal plain
    (all-purpose) flour, plus extra
    for dusting
1½ teaspoons instant dried yeast
2 teaspoons honey
1 cup (250 ml) warm water
1 tablespoon olive oil
3 tablespoons ghee
3 garlic cloves, crushed
1 teaspoon finely grated lemon zest
1 bunch coriander (cilantro),
    leaves chopped

1   Preheat the oven to 160°C (315°F).

2   Melt the ghee in a large ovenproof saucepan over medium–high heat. Season the lamb shanks with salt and freshly ground black pepper and brown well. Remove from the pan and set aside.

3   Cook the onion and eggplant in the same pan for a few minutes. Add the ginger, garlic and spices and cook for 2 minutes or until fragrant. Stir in the tomatoes, stock, coconut milk, chickpeas and honey. Return the lamb shanks to the pan, nestling them under the vegetables, and bring to the boil. Cover, transfer to the oven and bake for 2 hours. Add the cauliflower and cook for a final 30 minutes or until everything is meltingly tender.

4   Meanwhile, make the naan. Combine the flour, yeast and a generous pinch of salt in a large bowl. Dissolve the honey in the warm water, then add it to the flour along with the oil and stir to form a dough. Tumble the dough onto a floured surface and knead for a few minutes until smooth (add extra flour, little by little, if the dough is too sticky). Place the dough in a lightly oiled bowl. Cover with a clean, damp tea towel and set aside in a warm place for 45 minutes or until doubled in size.

5   Divide the dough into four balls. Stretch or roll a ball out into an oval about 5 mm (¼ inch) thick. Cook in a dry frying pan over medium heat for a few minutes, turning once, until puffed and lightly golden. Repeat with the remaining dough.

6   Melt the ghee with the garlic, lemon zest and some salt and pepper in a small saucepan. Brush the mixture over the cooked naan and sprinkle a little coriander over the top.

7   Sprinkle the remaining coriander over the curry and serve with the naan.

Glazed salmon with rice

Prep time: 10 minutes,
  plus marinating
Cook time: 15 minutes
Serves 2

¼ cup (60 ml) soy sauce
2 tablespoons sweet chilli sauce
1 tablespoon sesame oil
1 cm (½ inch) knob of ginger,
  grated
1 teaspoon black sesame seeds
2 garlic cloves, sliced
2 salmon fillets, skin on
Olive oil, for cooking
2 bok choy, leaves separated
2 cups (370 g) cooked
  basmati rice

When I was younger, I barely ate any fish or seafood (because I'd say it was 'fishy'). As I got older, I learned how great it is to have a variety of fish in my diet, so I had to come up with strong flavours that pair well, and this is perfect.

1   Add 2 tablespoons of the soy sauce to a bowl with the sweet chilli sauce, sesame oil, ginger, sesame seeds and half the garlic. Mix until well combined. Add the salmon to the bowl and turn to coat well. Marinate in the fridge for up to 1 hour if time permits.

2   Preheat the oven to 200°C (400°F). Line a baking tray with baking paper. Place the salmon on the tray, skin side down, and spoon the remaining marinade over the top. Bake for 12–15 minutes or until the salmon is cooked to your liking.

3   Meanwhile, heat a small splash of olive oil in a non-stick frying pan over medium heat. Add the bok choy and cook for 3–4 minutes or until slightly wilted. Add the remaining garlic and a sprinkle of salt and freshly ground black pepper and cook for another 3 minutes. Add the remaining soy sauce to the pan and mix well.

4   Serve the salmon on a bed of cooked basmati rice, topped with the bok choy.

Coconut rice

Prep time: 5 minutes
Cook time: 20 minutes
Serves 4–6 as a side

Olive oil, for cooking
½ small brown onion, diced
1 cm (½ inch) knob of ginger,
  thickly sliced
1 cup (200 g) jasmine rice,
  rinsed
1 cup (250 ml) vegetable stock
1 cup (250 ml) coconut milk

This rice is next level and will seriously elevate your rice game. It can be made in advance or you can make it as part of your meal prep so that it has time to develop even more flavour.

1 In a small saucepan with a lid, heat a small splash of olive oil over medium heat. Add the onion and ginger slices and cook for 3 minutes or until the onion is translucent.

2 Stir in the rice, add the stock and coconut milk and cover the pan. Bring to the boil, then turn down to a simmer and put a timer on for 15 minutes.

3 When the timer goes off, remove the pan from the heat and discard the ginger slices. Fluff the rice with a fork for extra-fluffy coconut rice.

Crispy garlic potatoes

Prep time: 15 minutes
Cook time: 1 hour
Serves 4–6 as a side

20 baby potatoes
⅓ cup (80 ml) olive oil
4 garlic cloves, thinly sliced
2 small red chillies, thinly sliced
4 rosemary sprigs, leaves picked
¼ cup basil leaves

This family favourite has my two favourite things: garlic and potatoes! These are the perfect side dish to accompany a roast dinner.

1 Preheat the oven to 180°C (350°F). Line a roasting tin with baking paper.

2 Add the whole potatoes to a large deep saucepan and cover with water. Cover and bring to the boil over high heat, then reduce the heat and simmer for 20–25 minutes. Drain well.

3 Meanwhile, add the olive oil, garlic, chilli, rosemary and basil to a frying pan. Cook over low heat for 5–7 minutes or until the garlic is lightly browned – keep an eye on it to ensure it doesn't burn. Set aside to cool slightly.

4 Strain the infused oil through a sieve and set it aside (the oil should have a deeper colour now). Tip the garlic, chilli and herb mixture onto a chopping board and finely chop it.

5 Transfer the boiled potatoes to the roasting tin. Using a flat spatula, press down on each potato, crushing it. Drizzle the infused oil over the potatoes and sprinkle with the garlic and herb mixture, ensuring each potato is completely coated. Season with salt and pepper and bake the potatoes for 30 minutes or until golden brown and crisp.

Tip: These are perfect when cooked in the oven, but I think they're even better in an air fryer. Boil the potatoes as above, but put them in an air fryer at 180°C (350°F) for 20 minutes for the final cooking.

Balsamic pumpkin

Prep time: 10 minutes
Cook time: 45 minutes
Serves 4 as a side

500 g (1 lb 2 oz) pumpkin
   (squash), skin on
2–3 tablespoons balsamic glaze
   (see Tip)
Olive oil, for drizzling
Large pinch of salt
Large pinch of freshly ground
   black pepper

It doesn't take much effort to turn basic roast pumpkin into a super-delicious side dish. Add a protein and salad of your choice. It goes really well with the Spicy beef roast (page 196).

1 Cut the pumpkin into large bite-sized pieces and add it to a large bowl. Drizzle the pumpkin with the balsamic glaze and olive oil and sprinkle with the salt and pepper. Mix well to completely coat the pumpkin.

2 Add the pumpkin to an air-fryer basket. Close the air fryer and turn it to 180°C (350°F) for 25 minutes. Alternatively, preheat the oven to 180°C (350°F) and cook the pumpkin in a roasting tin lined with baking paper for 45 minutes or until golden and tender.

Tip: Balsamic glaze is available in supermarkets. It's made by adding a little sugar to balsamic vinegar and cooking until it has reduced and thickened. Balsamic glaze is sweeter than balsamic vinegar, but they're both great!

Rosemary and olive flatbreads

Prep time: 15 minutes
Cook time: 25 minutes
Makes 6

2 cups (300 g) self-raising
    flour, plus extra for dusting
1½ cups (400 g) Greek-style
    yoghurt
1 tablespoon olive oil, plus extra
    for cooking
2 tablespoons dried rosemary
1–2 tablespoons Olive sprinkle
    (page 190)

These breads freeze well and are perfect to use as wraps or pizza bases, or to accompany curries. You can also serve them warm on a platter with dips (my favourite way to eat them!).

1   Mix the flour, yoghurt and olive oil in a bowl to make a sticky, crumbly dough. Knead the dough on a floured benchtop until it forms a ball. If it's still sticky, add some more flour.

2   Using a knife, split the dough into six portions and knead each portion into a ball. Roll out one of the balls with a rolling pin until about 1 cm (½ inch) thick. Scatter a sixth of the rosemary and olive sprinkle over the dough, then continue rolling until the dough is 5 mm (¼ inch) thick. Repeat with the remaining dough balls.

3   Heat a small splash of olive oil in a frying pan over medium heat. Add one of the flatbreads and cook for 2 minutes or until lightly browned, then flip and cook the other side. Remove from the pan and cook the remaining flatbreads, adding a little more oil if needed.

Basil pasta topper

Prep time: 5 minutes
Cook time: Nil
Serves 4

1 large bunch basil, leaves picked
1 garlic clove
1–2 tablespoons olive oil
Juice of ½ lemon

Spoon the basil paste over the top of your favourite pasta or use it on top of a lasagne to bring a real freshness to the meal. This can be frozen for up to 3 months.

1 On a large chopping board, finely chop the basil. It's best to do this by hand as the oils and juices will come out the more you cut.

2 Add the garlic and keep chopping until the garlic is finely chopped. Pour the olive oil and lemon juice over the top and continue chopping until the mixture resembles a chunky paste. Season with salt and pepper.

Acknowledgements

This book would not have been possible without the support and trust from **Murdoch Books**. I am so appreciative of the team for believing in us and helping every step of the way.

Thank you to my partner **Mitch**, who truly forever believes in me and everything we do together. Everything we do and succeed in together, is because you are the most selfless, genuine and supportive partner I could ever ask for, and I'm forever lucky to have you by my side every step of the way. We can tick book #2 off our bucket list, we did it!

Thank you to **my mum**, who is the most incredible, selfless and kind human being I know. I couldn't do half of the things I do without her help every day, and I couldn't thank her enough for all the support, recipe writing, late night editing and testing cook days that she does for us, all out of the kindness of her heart.

A loving thank you to **my grandparents**, who have instilled in me that fresh, colourful and tasty food is the way to go, and were really proud of our Greek heritage growing up – because I'm so lucky to be able to share it far and wide with recipes straight from their garden.

Finally, I am so appreciative of the **BARE community**, and those of you who love and support what we do every day. We wouldn't be here without you, and we are so thankful and appreciative of you.

Index

Published in 2022 by Murdoch Books, an imprint of Allen & Unwin

Murdoch Books Australia
83 Alexander Street
Crows Nest NSW 2065
Phone: +61 (0)2 8425 0100
murdochbooks.com.au
info@murdochbooks.com.au

Murdoch Books UK
Ormond House
26–27 Boswell Street
London WC1N 3JZ
Phone: +44 (0) 20 8785 5995
murdochbooks.co.uk
info@murdochbooks.co.uk

For corporate orders and custom publishing, contact our business development team at
salesenquiries@murdochbooks.com.au

Publisher: Jane Morrow
Editorial Manager: Justin Wolfers
Design Manager: Megan Pigott
Designer: Emily O'Neill
Editor: Justine Harding
Photographer: Ben Dearnley
Additional Photography: Frame Creative
Stylist: Vanessa Austin
Home Economist: Jacinta Cannataci
Food Assistant: Monica Cannataci
Production Director: Lou Playfair

*We acknowledge that we meet and work on the traditional lands of the Cammeraygal people
of the Eora Nation and pay our respects to their elders past, present and future.*

ISBN 978 1 92261 608 1 Australia
ISBN 978 1 91166 849 7 UK

A catalogue record for this
book is available from the
National Library of Australia

A catalogue record for this book is available
from the British Library

Colour reproduction by Splitting Image
Colour Studio Pty Ltd, Clayton, Victoria

Printed by Hang Tai Printing Company
Limited, China

OVEN GUIDE: You may find cooking times
vary depending on the oven you are using.
For fan-forced ovens, as a general rule,
set the oven temperature to 20°C (70°F)
lower than indicated in the recipe.

TABLESPOON MEASURES: We have used
20 ml (4 teaspoon) tablespoon measures.
If you are using a 15 ml (3 teaspoon)
tablespoon add an extra teaspoon of the
ingredient for each tablespoon specified.

10 9 8 7 6 5 4 3 2 1

FSC
www.fsc.org
MIX
Paper from
responsible sources
FSC® C023121